GREAT BRITISH
MOTOR CYCLES
OF THE THIRTIES

BOB CURRIE

IVY 🍂 LEAF

The publishers are grateful to the editor of
Motor Cycle Weekly for permission to reproduce
the majority of the black and white illustrations
in this book; to Manx Technical Publications and Bob Thomas
for the colour photograph of the Douglas Endeavour; and to
Andrew Morland for all the other colour photographs.

Originally published in 1981 by The Hamlyn Publishing Group Limited
part of Reed International Books

This edition published in 1991 by
Ivy Leaf
Michelin House
81 Fulham Road
London SW3 6RB

This edition produced exclusively for Bookmart Limited

ISBN 0 86363 038 3

Printed in Hong Kong

Contents

Introduction

Even now, there are those who imagine that motor cycle development came to a full stop stop at the end of the Golden Age of the 1920s, not to restart until the superbikes of the 1960s and 1970s came on the scene. Between lay nothing but a sea of grey porridge, lumpy with cheap-and-nasties, and with just a Brough Superior, or Ariel Square Four or two to provide the merest hint of cream.

It was not so, of course, as I hope this book makes abundantly clear. True there were, in Britain and Germany especially, economic and political pressures which affected the motor cycle to a considerable degree, and in consequence any survey of the motor cycling scene during the decade leading up to the Second World War must inevitably be something of a social history, too. Well, why not, anyway?

For my own part, the 1930s was a period in which I served my own motor cycling apprenticeship, progressing from schoolmates' machines (a round-tank BSA in a farmer's field, a front-wheel-drive Sheppee Cykelaid wobbling down a long drive now obliterated by the M5 Motorway) to the first machine that was truly my own – a 98 cc Excelsior Minor of 1931, bought third-hand for £3 10s, but in the eyes of a worrying mother a thing of monstrous power. A string of other models followed, the most costly being a 250 cc Rudge Radial bought from a London dealer's 'Postal Bargains' column in *Motor Cycling* for £9 10s. It arrived with a duff plug and a worn-out rear sprocket, and in consequence I have never again bought anything from that particular company; nor will I, for I have a very long memory.

In compiling this book I was fortunate in being able to draw on the personal memories of many active competitors of the time, in particular my near-neighbour, the late Harry Perrey. My thanks, also, to many others, who have reminisced with me of old times. They include Jackie Wood (one-time member of the British Army's trials and ISDT squad), Ginger Wood, Tyrell Smith, my journalistic colleague Vic Willoughby, and, especially, 'Mr BSA' himself, Bert Perrigo who was largely responsible for the section on trials.

Bob Currie

6

The slippery slope

Arlington Row, Bibury, Gloucestershire

There is ample reason why the 1920s are looked upon by motor cycle enthusiasts as a Golden Age, for this was the period during which the machine passed through adolescence and grew to adulthood. As the world struggled back to normality following the trauma of the First World War, so the demand arose for personal powered transport on a scale totally unknown in pre-war days.

But the bikes of 1919 were, in most instances, barely one step removed from the primitive. Certainly, rear-hub gears (a beefed-up version of those still current on pedal cycles) had given way to the more robust countershaft gearbox – with hand gear-change, of course – but especially in the lightweight field belt-drive was still almost universal. Front suspension was rudimentary; rear springing had made a tentative appearance, but was mistrusted by the general public. Engine lubrication was, in most cases, total-loss, and operated by a hand pump in or alongside the fuel tank, worked whenever the rider felt sufficiently brave as to risk taking one hand off the handlebar. Tyres were of narrow section, board-hard, and beaded edge.

Gradually, the new metals and techniques evolved in wartime were adapted to peacetime use. Competition work such as the Isle of Man TT races, and six day trials, led to the development of better tyres, frames, and suspension systems, and to more powerful and more reliable engines.

By 1930 (at the close of which year 'vintage' ended and 'post-vintage' began) the motor cycle had matured, and could boast of mechanical dry-sump oiling, fatter and more comfortable wired-edge tyres, a shapely saddle tank, electric instead of acetylene gas lighting, and on the more expensive models the benefits of rear springing and a foot-change gearbox. However, the machine had by no means reached the end of the line, and there was plenty of good stuff yet to come.

Britain, Germany, and to a lesser degree, France and Italy were the main motor cycling nations of the time, but across the Atlantic the motor cycle had almost died, killed off by the cheap, mass-produced car. Certainly there were some enthusiasts left who could appreciate such machines as the Indian Four, but the rival Henderson and Cleveland fours were about to die, leaving the two major American factories, Indian and Harley-Davidson, to rely principally on the manufacture of massive vee-twins for law-enforcement purposes.

A look at what the Paris Show of 1930 had to offer is interesting. From Motoconfort (today the manufacturer of Mobylette mopeds) there was a beautiful and highly-advanced four-in-line with shaft final drive. Two other four-cylinder machines were shown by Chaise (a 500 cc model with fan-assisted cooling) and Train (another shaft-drive mount with, unusually, an outside flywheel at the front of the power unit). The well-known Terrot company exhibited a neat semi-unit-construction single, with a cylindrical gearbox which could be rotated in its housing to adjust the primary chain (the same idea

America was the home of the straight-four, as typified by the Henderson, Cleveland, Pierce, and Ace. But Ace got into difficulties after designer Bill Henderson was killed while testing a prototype, and the firm was later bought-up by Indian. The 1930 Indian 4 employed the Ace engine in a typically Indian frame

was used in the 1960s on Matchless lightweights). An imposing Koehler-Escoffier featured a telescopic front fork. Aircraft-engine builders Gnôme et Rhone featured totally-enclosed valve gear on their massive transverse flat-twin.

All this was very impressive, but the bald truth was that France's total production of medium- and heavyweight motor cycles was relatively small, and under the heady froth was some very flat beer indeed in the form of a myriad of low-powered *vélomoteurs*, many of them little more than motorised bicycles. The explanation of the hordes of buzzy miniatures was that the enlightened French government permitted them to be used free of road tax.

In Britain, the outlook appeared especially bright as the doors of the Olympia exhibition hall swung open for the 1930 London Show. Major attractions were two ingenious four-cylinder machines. One was the 500 cc overhead-camshaft Ariel Square Four, on the development of which Edward Turner had spent the past couple of years. Its rival was the Matchless Silver Hawk, with an engine that looked not unlike that of the Ariel, but which was in fact a narrow-angle vee-four.

Those were by no means all the novelties. Back in June, Rudge-Whitworth, of Coventry had created a TT sensation by finishing 1-2-3 in the Junior TT with a new four-valve single in which the valves were arranged radially in a hemispherical cylinder head, valve operation being by way of two pushrods and a complicated system of rockers. Now, road-going counterparts of the Rudge Radial were on view.

Douglas had a new long and lithe 494 cc overhead-valve flat twin, and OK Supreme a sports-roadster version of their 'Lighthouse' vertical-camshaft, unit-construction racer. Dunelt, like Francis-Barnett, must have combed an ornithological dictionary to find names for their new 1931 range – although their choice of names was none too happy; there cannot have been many prospective customers attracted by the thought of riding around on a 350 cc ohv Dunelt Vulture, while the 500 cc Dunelt Drake sounded just a little too much like Donald Duck!

Enclosure of the engine and gearbox was the coming thing, reckoned a couple of factories. Triumph therefore exhibited two models with pressed-steel shields covering the lower parts of the assembly. Advantage claimed was that the bike could be cleaned in no time, just by giving it a swish down with a hose pipe (but the manufacturer had the greater gain, because he could dispense with the expensive business of polishing the more eye-catching bits of the crankcase and gearbox castings).

Sensibly, Triumph had done no more than dip their toes into the water, to test public reaction. More foolhardily, New Hudson leapt into the enclosure pool fully-clothed. For 1931, their entire existing range of machines had been scrapped and, in their place, a whole parade of newcomers – side-valve and overhead-valve, from 350 to 600 cc and encompassing sloggers, tourers, and sportsters – flaunted pressed-steel enclosure of the works.

Not only were there detachable bonnets covering the crankcase and gearbox, but the underside of the duplex frame was sheeted in too. A futuristic styling

theme, extending even to the shape of the front number plate, was common to the range, while gimmicks included a tank-top instrument facia, and a four-speed Moss gearbox of which the kick-starter crank when fully depressed served as a prop-stand.

The story behind this New Hudson metamorphosis was that a vigorous new broom, ex-Ariel executive Vic Mole, had taken over as managing director, and one of his first directives was that chief designer Arthur Woodman should revamp the catalogue completely. Woodman was certainly a competent designer (earlier, he had been responsible for the face-cam Chater-Lea and, later, he would be involved with Coventry-Eagle in the design of the rear-sprung, enclosed-engine Pullman model), but on this occasion Mole had asked him to do too much at one time.

Understandably, the New Hudsons were to run into a number of teething problems; word spread around among the motor cycling fraternity, and the factory found itself with a basketful of lemons. Committed to their programme, New Hudsons soldiered on for the next two years, but although the bugs were all eliminated in time, sales of the models plummetted. And when a Mr Girling came along, looking for somebody to manufacture his patented braking and suspension systems, New Hudson gladly packed in the motor cycle side and retooled the works.

Above: with the coming of the 1930s, the old-established New Hudson firm took a leap into the future with a completely new range of machines featuring enclosure of the crankcase and gearbox, inclined engines and a streamlined overall appearance. Unhappily the public didn't bite. Shown here is the 493 cc ohv Model 3 of 1932

Left: another model from the 'enclosed' New Hudson range, the 550 cc side-valve, carried out an observed test in which the machine was driven from Brooklands to Lands End and back 20 times without stopping the engine. The test, in May, 1931, gained the firm an ACU Certificate of Performance, but not the hoped-for Maude's Trophy

About a week before the opening of the 1930 London Show, Britain had regained the world speed record from Germany, Joe Wright having been timed at 150·73 mph along the Carrigrohane Straight, just outside Cork in Southern Ireland. Accordingly, when the Show opened, what was proclaimed to be the record-breaking machine was displayed under spotlights on the OEC stand. Powered by a vee-twin, supercharged, 998 cc JAP

engine, it was an imposing monster with the patented OEC Duplex front fork arrangement.

But within a day or two the rumours started flying around. Oh yes, Joe had broken the record – but not with *that* bike. Subsequent investigation by the ACU established that Wright had taken two blown 998 cc JAP-engined models with him to Cork, the reserve model being his Zenith with which he had earlier taken various national records. In the dawn light, he began his record run on the OEC, but then the engine-shaft sprocket key sheared, and he had to bring out the reserve model instead. It was the Zenith which took the record.

Why the Showtime substitution? That was never satisfactorily explained, but suspicion was rife. As Zenith, at that time, were temporarily out of

Scandal of the 1930 Olympia Show was the exhibition on the OEC stand of a blown vee-twin with which, it was claimed, Joe Wright had set a new world speed record of 150·736 mph. The record was genuine enough, but Wright had in fact used another machine for the attempt after the OEC had packed up. The real record-breaker was a supercharged 996 cc Zenith, and in this picture, never before published, he is seen preparing the machine in his private workshop

production (they restarted, under new management, a few months later), it was felt that it would be better to advertise the bike as being the product of an existing factory.

Yet for all the promise of that 1930 London Show, the year ahead was to prove a traumatic one for the motor cycle industry, not only in Britain but world wide. For the underlying reason goes back to October, 1929, and to the United States. In the late 1920s a vast number of Americans had caught the Stock Exchange gambling fever and, urged on by unscrupulous promoters, had plunged into scatter-brained speculation.

Something had to give. Late in 1929 the bubble burst, share prices hit the slippery slope, and panic-stricken small investors clamoured for their money back. Banking houses just did not have the cash on hand to answer the calls and, one by one, they slammed the doors. Paper fortunes were wiped out in a single day, and the suicide rate rocketed.

But Wall Street had been responsible also for overseas investment, and for the supply of money to other countries. When the bottom fell out of the

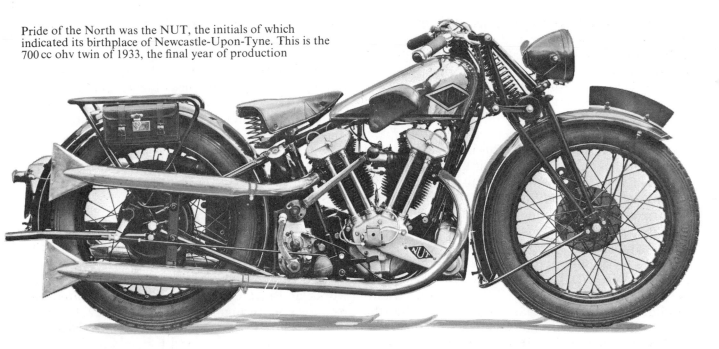

Pride of the North was the NUT, the initials of which indicated its birthplace of Newcastle-Upon-Tyne. This is the 700 cc ohv twin of 1933, the final year of production

market the effect on international trade was calamitous and, within two years, this was to be slashed by half. Especially hard hit were the economies of Austria and Germany (in the latter country, unemployment soared to over 5,000,000) and it was because of this state of financial chaos that Adolf Hitler and the Nazi Party gained ground so rapidly.

Nor could Britain escape. London, like New York, was an international banking centre, and the collapse of the dollar led in turn to a run on sterling and, eventually, to abandonment of the gold standard. Britain's unemployment figure reached 2,000,000 and at that level it was to stay until, in the latter part of the decade, national unease fostered by Hitler's activities brought a rearmament programme.

However, that was to come, and the Great Depression led to wholesale slaughter among the smaller companies of the British motor cycle industry. Of those marques active (though in some cases, only just) in 1930, the names of AKD, Chater-Lea, Diamond, Dot, Grindlay-Peerless, Ivy, LGC, New Comet, New Henley, New Gerrard, New Hudson, NUT, P & P, Radco, Rex-Acme, and Sharratt had all dropped out within the next two or three years.

Not all sank without trace, of course, and some are still alive in 1980, albeit in other fields. Abingdon King Dick, who in 1930 were offering a range of extremely neat little four-stroke lightweights of their own design, were primarily manufacturers of spanners and hand tools; motor cycles were abandoned, and the tools business expanded, after the company

was taken over by Bill Mansell, previously a director of Nortons.

The Chater-Lea, New Comet (Haden Bros.) and Radco firms today make components for the bicycle and motor cycle trade as, indeed, they always had. Dunelt simply closed down the motor cycle workshop and got on with their main line of business, the production of the special steels for which they are famous. Sharratt's of West Bromwich became important car dealers. Len Gundle, who produced the LGC, carried on with butcher-boy tradesmens' cycles and ice-cream tricycles. Diamond opted for car trailers and pedestrian-controlled milk floats.

Two of the saddest total casualties in the list, however, were Rex-Acme and NUT. Only three years before, Rex-Acme had been prominent in road-racing, with TT and Brooklands successes, with the great Wal Handley in charge of the competitions department. But by 1930 the skids were under the company. The long-established works at Earlsdon, Coventry, closed, and Rex-Acme merged with sidecar builders Mills-Fulford Ltd. But that partnership was of short duration, and before long Rex-Acme had disappeared, taking Mills-Fulford with it.

The NUT initials stood for Newcastle-upon-Tyne, where a strikingly handsome series of vee-twin roadsters, of 500, 700 and 750 cc, was built.

Founded by Hugh Mason, NUT had got away to a flying start by winning the 1911 Junior TT, and with the financial backing of the Sir Angus Sanderson group, reached a production peak in the early 1920s. But the withdrawal of capital in favour of the

then-new Angus Sanderson car left the firm out on a limb. By 1932 NUT were leading a bare existence by selling bikes, a handful at a time, through one London outlet. The next year was the final one.

New Henley's story was something else again. Originally a Birmingham-based outfit, they had specialised in super-sporting singles, but an incompetent and profligate management left the company in a very rocky state as the 1920s ran to a close. But at that point a New Henley fanatic known as Johnny ('Mad Jack') Crump, had a windfall in the shape of a substantial legacy from his grandmother. With this he bought the moribund New Henley firm and restarted production in part of the one-time Bradbury premises at Wellington Works, Oldham. Assisted by Arthur Greenwood, Crump thrived for a short while, even to the extent of running official New Henley entries in the TT races. But grandmothers' legacies do not last for ever, and when the money finally ran out, that was the end of the tale.

However, the smaller firms were by no means the only ones to feel the financial draught. Some of the most illustrious names of all – like AJS, Ariel, New Imperial, Sunbeam, Rudge, and Triumph – were

able to survive to the end of the decade only because of lifelines thrown from outside.

Founded by the four Stevens brothers (Jack, Joe, George, and Harry), AJS of Wolverhampton ran into the most appalling slice of bad luck. There had been nothing wrong with the AJS operation, and until the slump things were going swimmingly. But the bad luck was that the brothers had chosen to expand at quite the wrong period in time. To the output of motor cycles had been added the AJS Light 10 car (derived from the extinct Clyno), the AJS Pilot motor coach chassis, and even radio sets – the range of which was headed by the console Symphony Seven, with the familiar AJS monogram incorporated in the fretted plywood of the loudspeaker front.

Such an expansion, which included an additional works at Bilston, stretched the Stevens' financial resources to twanging point, and by 1931 it was known that AJS had run into big trouble. Negotiations were put in hand for a merger with BSA, but these came to nothing. Instead, it was Matchless who stepped in to purchase the manufacturing rights and goodwill of AJS motor cycles, while Willys-Overland-Crossley took over the building of the AJS Light 10 car.

Ironically, when the liquidator had sold off all the various bits and pieces of the old AJS company, it became clear that the problem had been one that

An enterprising AJS design was this transverse vee-twin 500 cc of 1931, produced just before liquidation of the Wolverhampton plant. Tooling and manufacturing rights were sold to Japan, where some were built by a local company immediately prior to the Second World War

today would be termed 'cash flow'. That the concern had been basically sound was evident from the fact that all creditors were paid the full twenty shillings in the pound and, moreover, the Stevens brothers still owned the original factory at Retreat Street, Wolverhampton, where they had begun the AJS business back in 1910.

Throughout 1931, the overall situation deteriorated rapidly. France and Germany both decided to abandon the idea of motor cycle shows, and only Britain and Italy elected to go ahead. Even at that, BSA opted out of Olympia. Instead, the 1932 range,

Top: in the worst year of the depression, 1932, the annual London Show was cancelled and, instead, the larger dealers staged their own displays of the new-season's models. This is Godfrey's of London, with a special showing of all the 1933 Brough Superior (foreground) and BSA (background) models. Factory personnel were in attendance, too

Above: the depressed market caused George Brough to build what was to be the smallest-capacity Brough Superior ever marketed. It was a 498 cc ohv twin, equipped with the new and lighter Brampton-Monarch front fork, and reputedly capable of 80 to 85 mph. Nine were built, the first being despatched in January, 1931, and three are known to survive

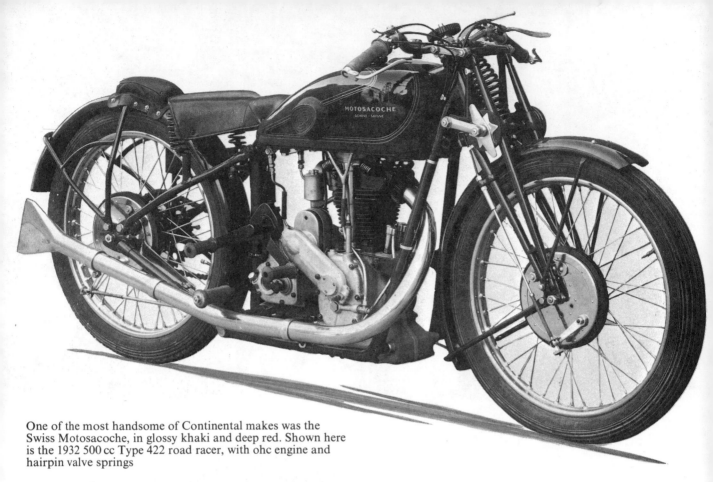

One of the most handsome of Continental makes was the Swiss Motosacoche, in glossy khaki and deep red. Shown here is the 1932 500 cc Type 422 road racer, with ohc engine and hairpin valve springs

which included a new range of sports models known as the Blue Stars, with tuned engines and upswept exhaust pipes, were exhibited first at a dealer convention at the Small Heath factory, then transferred to major showrooms around the country, one of these being Godfrey's of London. The competitions Blue Star was derived from the works

model campaigned in trials and scrambles by Bert Perrigo, and in recognition BSA paid Bert the princely royalty of one halfpenny for each one sold. Still, in 1932 even an extra couple of shillings a week was not to be sneezed at . . .

There was a kind of piquancy in the fact that as the stand fitters were at work preparing for the 1931

Four-valve engines became a fashion in the early 1930s, sparked off by Rudge racing success. Ariel climbed on the band-wagon with the 1931 497 cc Model SG31 sloper, a design by Val Page, but because of financial troubles the factory had to trim the programme. The frame of the SG31 was used, also, for the overhead-camshaft Square Four

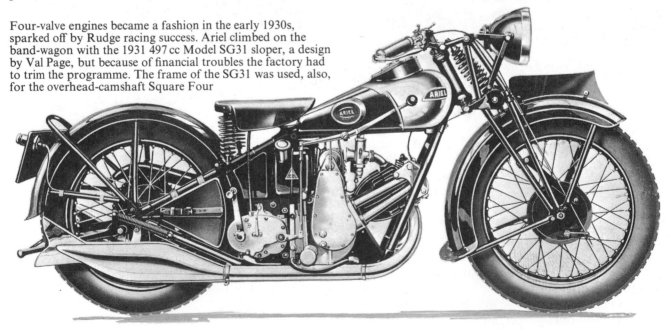

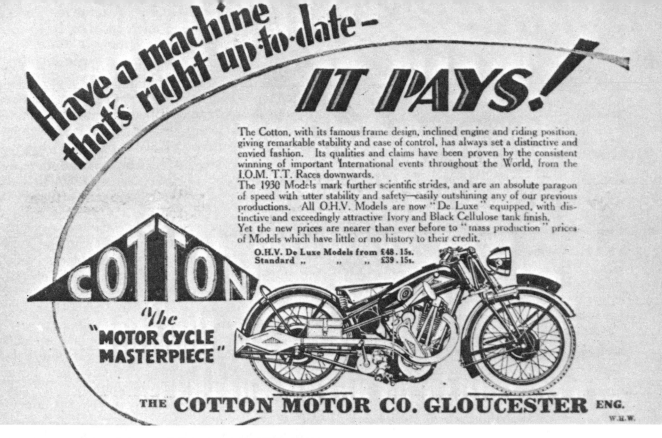

London Show, so a fleet of lorries was trundling down the A5 highway, carrying the parts and equipment from the now-closed Graiseley Works of AJS down to the Matchless works at Woolwich. Although, so far as the general public was concerned, AJS was an absentee from Olympia, in fact a projected 1932 AJS was shown to dealers visiting the office part of the Matchless stand.

It was an intriguing Show, for all that. As always, George Brough had prepared a crowd stopper, and this time it took the form of an 800 cc water-cooled four (the engine was a specially-enlarged Austin Seven) with shaft drive which passed between twin rear wheels. In the course of time ten Brough-Austins were to be built, and several still survive in the hands of enthusiasts.

Ariel had an exciting new 500 cc sports single with a four-valve upright engine, and for this newcomer they had chosen the catchy name of Red Hunter. There were other duplex-frame models, housing two-valve and four-valve engines so inclined as to be not far short of horizontal, and a 600 cc version of the Square Four.

From Velocette came the 250 cc two-stroke Model GTP, first seen a year earlier, but now equipped with a proportionally-variable pumped lubrication system linked directly to the throttle-slide opening. Many years later, Japanese manufacturers were to claim Posi-Force oiling as a new invention!

Formerly concentrating their efforts on the 350 cc Ivory Calthorpe only (possibly the most aesthetic-

15

Above: in 1930 there were two British entries for the four-cylinder field, from Ariel and Matchless. Here Arthur Bourne ('Torrens', columnist and editor of *The Motor Cycle*) poses with the overhead-camshaft Matchless Silver Hawk, a narrow-angle vee-four. Eventual winner of the battle was the Ariel Square Four

Below: it was rare to find a company offering a catalogued competitions machine (most competition bikes were adapted roadsters) but Triumph, in 1932, listed this 493 cc Model CD Competitions, with upswept exhaust system, sump undershield, Bowden carburettor, and ball-bearing rocker gear

ally pleasing design of its time), Calthorpe now added 250 cc two-stroke and 500 ohv Ivory models to the range. And the impending change in taxation accounted for several new machines aimed at taking advantage of a clause permitting models weighing less than 224 lb (previously it had been a 200 lb limit) to be taxed at only £1 10s (£1·50p) per year. To devise an under-224 lb 500 cc was something of an achievement, but both Douglas and Matchless had managed it.

But for all the glamour of the new-season's models, the drop in attendance at Olympia – only 68,000 visitors, as compared with 107,000 in 1930 – was ominous. One of the two British weekly journals covering the two-wheel field, *Motor Cycling*, put the general feeling into words. 'The year 1931,' commented an editorial feature, 'has been, in everyday language, a flop. Several of our great manufacturers are reporting that they have done less than half the trade they expected. From every centre where motor cycles have been sold in large numbers in the past has come the same story – nobody has any money.'

That applied also to Britain's traditional export markets, and some countries were now so short of sterling that they would pay for imports in their own currency only, or with goods in kind. Because of this, some motor cycle factories found themselves paid off in cocoa beans, or native-made carpets, which they then had to dispose of through the home market. Still, as *Motor Cycling* was to remark: 'Our manufacturers are showing the world that they can trim their sails for stormy weather, with no less skill

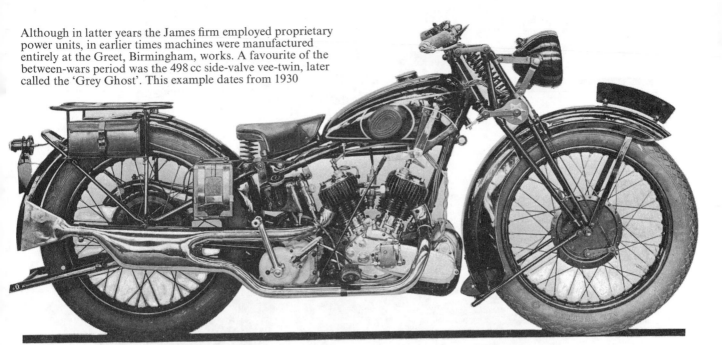

Although in latter years the James firm employed proprietary power units, in earlier times machines were manufactured entirely at the Greet, Birmingham, works. A favourite of the between-wars period was the 498 cc side-valve vee-twin, later called the 'Grey Ghost'. This example dates from 1930

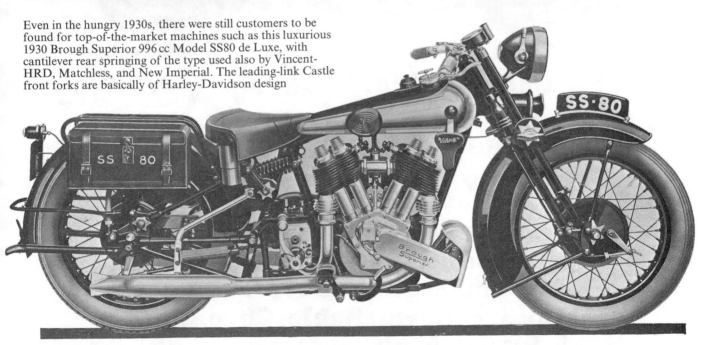

Even in the hungry 1930s, there were still customers to be found for top-of-the-market machines such as this luxurious 1930 Brough Superior 996 cc Model SS80 de Luxe, with cantilever rear springing of the type used also by Vincent-HRD, Matchless, and New Imperial. The leading-link Castle front forks are basically of Harley-Davidson design

than for the fine trade winds that were blowing a year or two ago.' Stirring words but, unhappily, trimming the sails was by no means as easy as all that.

One concern that had developed a very large export trade over the years was Ariel, based at Selly Oak, Birmingham. Collapse of this section of their business left Ariel in a very precarious position and, in 1932, they ceased trading. But Jack Sangster, the managing director, was certainly not content to stand aside and watch the company go to the wall. He, and his father Charles before him, had been in

charge of Ariel since the late 1890s, and now Jack went into action, cramming key pieces of production equipment into a smaller part of the former premises, and wheeling and dealing wherever he could.

Essential staff, sacked when Ariel Motors collapsed, were re-engaged (although at a reduction in salary) and, by throwing his personal fortune into the coffers, Jack Sangster got Ariel back into production under the new name of Ariel Works (JS) Ltd. The 'JS' initials were indicative of his own involvement.

Matchless
IN NAME & REPUTATION

The Matchless "X/2"

The only "Big Twin" in the World which has . . . . .

Dry Sump Lubrication . . .
Enclosed Valves . . . . .
Detachable Cylinder Head . .
Interconnected Brakes . . .
Duplex Trussed Loop Frame .
and Untarnishable Chromium Plated Finish . .
— all for £60

Matchless Model "X/2" 9·9 h.p. Solo (to standard specification)

£60

HIRE PURCHASE TERMS.
Model "X/2"
(to standard specification)
£15 DOWN
and 12 monthly payments of £4 14s. 9d. including Comprehensive Insurance Policy.

The Model "X/R2" is similar to the Model "X/2" but includes a sports engine with plated cylinders and polished valve ports, and chromium plated wheels.   Price to standard specification £62 10s.

•   •   •

Write for the Matchless Introductory Catalogue and the "Silver Arrow" Folder.

MATCHLESS MOTORCYCLES
(COLLIERS) LTD.
44–45, Plumstead Road,
Plumstead, London, S.E.18.
Phone: Woolwich 1010 (4 lines).
Grams: "Matchless, Woolwich."

All "Matchless" Motor-cycles are fitted with
STURMEY ARCHER 3 SPEED GEAR

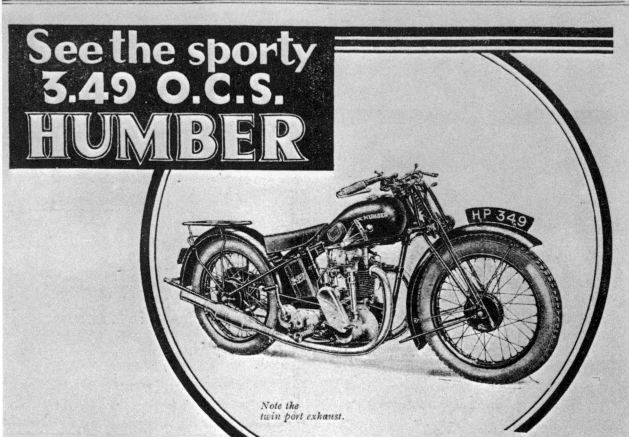

See the sporty 3.49 O.C.S. HUMBER

Note the twin port exhaust.

See the 1930 Overhead Camshaft Humber with twin port exhaust—you will like its sporty appearance—lively engine, high turn of speed, graceful lines and comfortable low riding position. The O.C.S. model conforms to the famous Humber standard—every part is of the highest possible quality.

Furthermore, it is available on the easiest of easy payment systems, which includes a most comprehensive Insurance policy.

Call round at your dealer's. Inspect this and other Humber models. The O.H.V. (push rod type) at £48 is sure to interest you.

HUMBER LTD. COVENTRY

Price
£56
or
£4 - 6 - 0
a month.

CUT THIS OUT.

Please send me—FREE—Motor Cycle catalogue and full particulars of Humber models.

NAME ....

ADDRESS ....

....

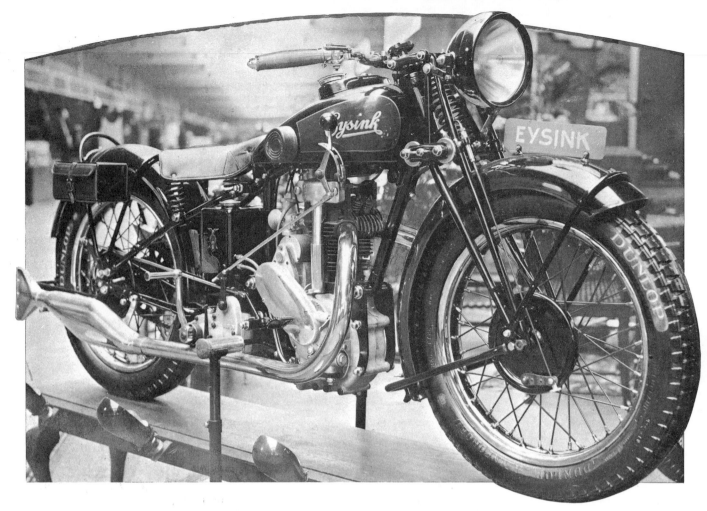

Rudge were perpetually in money troubles, and to gain extra revenue, they sold their four-valve engines to other makers, at home and abroad, using a Python trade-mark. This is the 1931 Dutch-built Eysink-Python 499 cc four valver

However, the lengthy Ariel programme was pruned drastically, with only two basic frame designs covering the entire production of 250, 350 and 500 cc singles, and the 600 cc Square Four.

As mentioned a little while earlier, the only other nation to stage a full-scale Show was Italy. 'We must watch Italy,' warned *Motor Cycling*, in December 1931, 'She has forged ahead in sport and is forging ahead in manufacture.'

For one thing, it was rare to find a head of state who was a confirmed motor cycling enthusiast, but Benito Mussolini, 'Il Duce' of the Fascisti and virtual dictator of Italy, was the proud holder of membership card No. 1 of the Moto-Club Italia, and a huge blow-up of Mussolini riding his 175 cc Bianchi dominated the Bianchi stand. Indeed, many stands exhibited 175 cc models (some of them of quite advanced design, with overhead camshaft engines) and the reason for this was that Italy had freed up-to-175 cc models from road tax, in much the same way that Germany did not demand tax on

under-200 cc machines.

But the Italian Show was not all small stuff, and a major highlight was a new racing Moto Guzzi across-the-frame four, with Cozette supercharger. It was reputed to develop 49 bhp, and to have lapped the Monza circuit during its development stage at 107 mph.

With the examples of France, Italy and Germany before them, was there no way the British Government could be persuaded to remove road tax from at least the smaller-capacity machines, so giving the motor cycle industry a much-needed boost? Representatives of the industry lobbied their Members of Parliament, and at one time it seemed possible that the newly-installed Labour Government would relent, at least to the extent of allowing up-to-125 cc bikes to be free from road tax.

That very faint hope caused the bike makers to beat a pathway to the door of Villiers, the Wolverhampton builders of proprietary two-stroke engines, demanding supplies of the 98 cc Villiers Midget engine previously employed in small lawnmowers.

First to rush out a 98 cc poverty model was Excelsior, in March, 1931. Listed as the Excelsior

Minor, it was a simple little machine with a single loop frame from the top tube of which there hung a triangular fuel tank formed from two edge-welded pressings. The gearbox was a two-speed Albion with the unexpected refinement of a foot-change pedal on the left. Actually, it was a heel-and-toe pedal, pivoted on the footrest hanger. Press the toe part down for top, the heel part down for bottom, and to obtain neutral the pedal should be left horizontal. Price, including direct electric lighting, was only £14 10s (£14·50p), which made it the cheapest true motor cycle in the whole history of the movement.

For all its diminutive size, the Excelsior Minor was a sturdy little bike, well able to carry the author and his brother at a speed of 25 mph, and capable of giving day-in, day-out loyalty.

Excelsior's bargain-basement Minor was quickly followed by a spate of competing machines, each powered by the same 98 cc Villiers engine, from Sun, Dot, Wolf, and Coventry-Eagle. Even the giant Triumph company joined in, with a simple underslung-tank model looking very much like the little Excelsior; but Triumph did have the shame-facedness to market it under the Gloria trade-mark, that being the name of their second-string bicycle company. Nobody could get down to Excelsior's price, and most were around £15 to £16. Classiest looker was the Dot, which boasted a saddle tank, but with electric lighting that machine worked out at 17 guineas (£17·85p).

In all of these, the final price included the dealer's profit, so it can be seen that the actual manufacturer was making pennies only on each bike built. With the bigger factories, concerned only in keeping their premises occupied, this did not matter overmuch. But it was life-or-death for a firm such as Dot, and old-established Lancashire dealers can still recall the time when Dot would build two or three bikes, then have to hawk them around on a trailer from showroom to showroom, selling them for cash with which to pay that week's wages bill. By 1933, Dot had ceased production and not until a reconstituted company secured a wartime Ministry of Food contract for Villiers-engined delivery three-wheelers did the name return to the motor cycle fold.

The industry's appeal for the lifting of road tax on the smallest capacity models failed to achieve its end, but Chancellor of the Exchequer Philip Snowden was able to give the bike makers a small concession by reducing the tax on under-150 cc machines to 15s (75p) a year, with effect from New Year's Day, 1932. It was something, if not as much as they had hoped for.

Belgium's premier manufacturer was FN (or in full, Fabrique Nationale des Armes de Guerre), primarily an armaments firm still famous for automatic weapons. The picture shows a nicely-restored 1933 500 cc side-valve unit-construction model. The FN tank badge is a stylised representation of a rifle on which is superimposed a bicycle crank and pedals, indicating the two sides of the factory's production

Encouragement for tiddlers

Jones Minor could well have described the passing of the Road Traffic Act of 1 December, 1930 as a rotten swizz. For ever since he could remember, the minimum age for holding a motor cycle driving licence had been 14 years; but now it was to be raised to 16 years in one jump, and the fact that boys who had already held a licence for more than six months would be allowed to carry on riding was but little consolation.

Yet should the thought of 14-year-old motor cyclists conjure up the image of rorty big Brough-Superior twins and the like, under the vestigial control of mere slips of lads in school caps, striped blazers, and grey flannel shorts, then forget it.

Truth was, very few schoolboys were in receipt of sufficient pocket money to afford anything more powerful than a fifth-hand 150 cc Francis-Barnett, a wee Levis, or just possibly an elderly Round Tank BSA. Even at that, with petrol costing as much as 1s 3d (6p) a gallon, use of the machine had to be rationed very carefully.

No, it was the principle of the thing that hurt, rather than the actuality. Jones Minor wondered if his schoolboy journalist hero, Falshaw Junior of *The Motor Cycle* (better known nowadays as *Daily Express* strip cartoonist, Barry Appleby) would have anything to say on the subject in the next issue of the magazine.

But the raising of the licence age was just one aspect of the 1930 Road Traffic Act, and there were many other clauses which affected the motor cyclist to a greater or lesser degree. The most important of these, possibly, decreed that henceforth every rider must take out compulsory insurance, at least against the possibility of third-party claims. That was fair enough, because an uninsured motor cyclist involved in a collision could well have found himself made bankrupt by a civil action for damages.

A cause for general celebration was the abolition of the overall 20 mph speed limit with effect from 1 January, 1931. As *The Motor Cycle* issue of that day commented; 'Today the Speed Limit dies its long-delayed death, and it is a case of "go as fast as you please", so long as you – and the general public – are safe in the eyes of the police.' Yes, that last phrase

was the sting in the tail, because the Act introduced the offence of 'careless driving', leaving it to the police to interpret that as they may.

What else? Well, the official ban on speed trials, hill climbs and races from the public highway was unlikely to upset the enthusiast very much. The time when such events were common had long since passed, most clubs imagined that there had been a ban in existence since the mid-1920s and, in any case, the growth of everyday traffic was in itself an inhibiting factor. Agreed, trials organisers had been in the habit of holding 'special tests' (usually a stop-and-restart, or a brake test) on convenient bits of roadway, mainly to resolve possible ties; but there was no reason why other tie-deciders, on private ground, could not be substituted.

Driving licence application forms would now have sections, which must be completed by the applicant, certifying his ability to read a registration number at a distance of 25 yards, and declaring that he was in sound health.

The final important stipulation was that, henceforth, a passenger could be carried only if the machine was fitted with 'a proper pillion' and with pillion footrests firmly attached to the frame. What constituted a 'proper pillion' was left for later interpretation, but one thing was clear – the happy-go-lucky practice of tying a loose cushion to the machine's rear carrier, and expecting Cicely or Jennifer to make the best of it, was definitely out! In due course the rider visiting his nearest accessory shop could choose between majestic 'proper pillions' like miniature spring mattresses, or horsehair-padded, leatherette-covered bricks which bolted to, or clipped to the edge of, the rear mudguard. Naturally, most riders opted for the horsehair bricks; they were cheaper.

Although not directly connected with the Road Traffic Act, another 1930 move was the establishment of a force of mobile police, usually mounted on solo motor cycles, although London chose to supplement its force of BSA Sloper-mounted mobiles, by cops travelling about in pairs in front-wheel-drive BSA three-wheelers (and it must be said that the three-wheelers were not universally popular

Dittisham, on the River Dart, Devonshire

The year 1930 saw the foundation of the London Metropolitan Police motor cycle patrols, especially for traffic-control duties. Machines used were 493 cc ohv BSA Slopers, supplemented by BSA three-wheelers

among the men in blue; the reason was that the front brake acted not on the wheels but on the front-drive differential, and any sudden brake application on the wet wood-block roads of the day could cause the trike to go into a Viennese waltz).

Sidecar outfits, with a speedometer mounted on the bodywork in such a way that it could be seen by both rider and passenger (who could therefore provide 'corroboration') were adopted by other forces. Choice of make was left to the force concerned, and local loyalties soon became evident. Birmingham settled for BSAs, Coventry for Triumphs, Worcestershire for Royal Enfields, and so on.

The next major piece of legislation affecting the motor cyclist came with the 1931 budget speech of Chancellor of the Exchequer Philip Snowden. This was the concession of a 15s annual tax for up-to-150 cc machines, to come into effect from 1 January,

1932. 'This,' hoped Mr Snowden, 'would give the hard-pressed industry assistance, by stimulating the use of ultra-lightweights such as the pedal-assisted models, costing around £12, so frequently seen on the roads of France.' Well, maybe; but those *bicyclettes a moteur* not only were relieved of road tax completely, but their riders did not even have to register them. It was just a matter of walking into a dealer's shop, handing over a wodge of francs, and riding off into the sunset without further formality. Whatever bureaucrats may think, the general public is allergic to form-filling, and the imposition of *any* tax – even one as low as this – would be a fetter on sales.

The same Snowden budget raised the concessionary weight for a £1 10s (£1·50p) annual tax from 200 to 224 lb, at the same time cutting the tax on an under-224 lb sidecar outfit – and there cannot have been many of those around – to £2 10s (£2·50p) annually. The key point was that the budget had introduced the principle of taxation by engine capacity, not overall weight, and that could be construed as a good thing. Although a 500 cc

Best-seller of the unit-construction New Imperial range was the 146 cc Unit Minor, in a sense the 'Honda 50' of its day. Thousands were used for workaday duties, but the versatile unit was used also for trials, road racing, and even speed record attempts! This is the 1935 de Luxe, with Lucas coil ignition, at £32

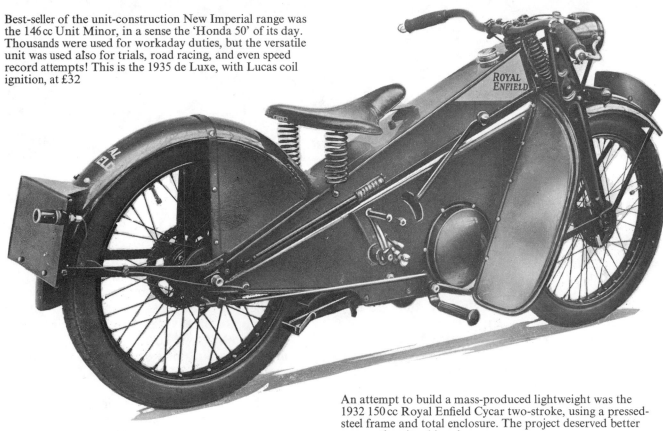

An attempt to build a mass-produced lightweight was the 1932 150 cc Royal Enfield Cycar two-stroke, using a pressed-steel frame and total enclosure. The project deserved better success than it achieved

Effective from 1 January, 1932, was a road tax concession for under-150 cc models. To bring home to the public the advantages a small machine could offer, the ACU staged a Lightweight Demonstration Run – in effect, a sales tour of the main towns of southern England – in which a convoy including the products of most British manufacturers took to the road. Here the parade has halted, in April, 1932, in an alleyway off High Street, Luton

machine weighing under 224 lb may sound to be a good deal, in order to get down to that weight a designer would have been tempted to use lighter components than would have been ideal.

In any case, by the time the next budget came around the idea of taxation by engine capacity would have been accepted in full, and the 224 lb concession would no longer be necessary. Nevertheless, once a machine had been taxed under the weight concession, prior to 1933, that would hold good for all time. Owners of vintage machines should note that it is still applicable, for which reason the author's own 1923 350 cc Dot is classed for taxation purposes as a 250 cc model.

Naturally, the announcement of the lower tax on under-150 cc models again caused manufacturers to stampede towards Wolverhampton, and the works of the Villiers Engineering Company. The result was a second crop of hastily-designed lightweights, this time with 150 cc two-stroke engines (although Cotton struck out in a new direction by introducing a one-mouse-power model featuring a 150 cc side-valve JAP engine).

Meanwhile, the major factories handed their design staffs the job of producing something a little more sophisticated within the 150 cc bracket. This

could not be done overnight, of course, but before very long some very attractive little 150 cc overhead-valve models began to appear on the market. One of the first (as might be expected by now) was an Excelsior, utilising an oil-in-sump sloper engine designed exclusively for the Birmingham company by Ike Hatch, and produced at the Blackburne works, in Surrey. A pretty little job with a red-panelled, chromium-plated tank, it should have sold well, but in fact only 200 were produced.

Rather better luck befell the Triumph contribution, the Model XO with inclined engine and angled

cylinder finning, housed in a simple duplex-loop welded frame. Then there was BSA, whose offering was a slightly scaled-down version of their 250 cc overhead-valve maid of all work; this was lively enough, and in post-war years the little BSA (sleeved down to 125 cc) was still competitive in 125 cc-class trials and scrambles.

Two of the new breed of one-fifties, however, stood head and shoulders above the rest, and should be given special mention. These were the Royal Enfield Model T, and the New Imperial Unit Minor.

Looking rather larger than it actually was, the Royal Enfield was a wonderfully compact little bike, and it introduced to the Redditch-built range the cast-in pushrod tunnels in cylinder block and head that were to become so familiar in later days. Oil was carried in a crankcase extension, valve gear was totally enclosed by a rocker cover secured by a single nut, and the four-speed gearbox could be supplied, at extra cost, in foot-change form.

Like the BSA, a few surviving Model T Enfields

Inspiration behind this streamlined, supercharged SS100 Brough Superior was all-Australian. The machine is Leaping Lena, and the intention was that owner Arthur Simcock (*right*) should use it to attempt the solo land speed record, while Alan Bruce (*second from left*) would fit a sidecar and go for the three-wheel records. Designer of the light-alloy shell was Phil Irving (*second from right*), and Keith Horton (*left*) assisted in preparation. The machine failed to get the solo record but Alan Bruce, in 1932, took Leaping Lena to a new sidecar record of 124·4 mph

were sleeved down for 125 cc-class sport in post-war years – a couple of them even came to the line in the first Ultra-Lightweight 125 cc TT races.

But of all the little 150 cc ohv models brought into being as the result of the 1931 budget, the one which stood out above the rest was the 146 cc New Imperial Unit Minor. Not only did it remain in production until the very last day of peace in 1939, but many examples were to give faithful service to those engaged on munitions work, right through the war years.

In fact, New Imperial were first in the field with an overhead-valve tiddler, the first Unit Minor sharing stand space at the 1931 Olympia Show with two more unit-construction machines from the same makers, of 350 and 500 cc; not only that, but the two larger models featured cantilever-type rear suspension on the Bentley and Draper principle.

The rear end of the little one-fifty was rigid (and for £28 10s, a customer could not reasonably have expected anything else) while Webb girder forks with pressed-steel blades looked after the front end. The actual capacity was only 138 cc, the pushrods ran up the rear of the cylinder and were operated by a transverse camshaft driven from the intermediate of the three gears which formed the primary drive.

Most unusually, ignition and lighting were provided by a Villiers flywheel magneto on the right of the engine mainshaft, which meant that there was an idle spark on the exhaust stroke. The final eccentricity was a three-speed gearbox operated by a long car-type joystick.

At the Show, New Imperial salesmen gathered in orders by the bushel, but back at the factory in Spring Road, Hall Green, Birmingham, out-and-out panic reigned. The bald truth was that the new ultra-lightweight would not pull the skin from even a lightly cooked rice pudding. Something had to be done, and pretty rapidly at that.

Incredibly, a totally new unit was designed, developed, and put into production in double-quick time, and by March, 1932, the bike was coming off the assembly line. Even more incredibly, New Imperial had managed to knock the retail price down slightly, and so the waiting customers found that they now had to pay only £28 7s (£28·35p).

The frame was the same, but the engine-gear unit in no way resembled the Olympia Show job. Gone was the Villiers flywheel magneto. Gone, too, was the intermediate gear of the primary drive and now there were just two primary-drive pinions with helical-cut teeth, and that meant that the engine 'ran backwards'. A third pinion, meshing with the clutch gear, drove a direct-current generator (dynamo)

Although intended as a cheap utility model, the 146 cc ohv New Imperial Unit Minor turned out to be a tough little cookie indeed. Not only did it amass many trials cups, but in August, 1935, Dorking dealer Harry Nash sleeved one to 123 cc, fitting it with a light-alloy fairing, and broke the world 125 cc flying-kilometer record at 70·101 mph. Happily, the machine is still in existence

with a contact-breaker assembly located at the far end. The capacity had risen to 146 cc, and valve operation was by pushrods located (in tubes) in the conventional manner on the right. A three-speed gearbox was retained, but instead of the joystick there was a normal (for the period) hand lever at the side of the fuel tank.

Rush job it may have been, but this time New Imps had got it right, and the sturdy little model was to be changed only slightly over the seven years ahead. In production form it offered a top speed of around 50 mph. Reliability was first class and, in a sense, it gave the artisan of the 1930s the same kind of service as does a Honda or Yamaha step-through today.

But, as might be expected, a more sporty section of the motor cycling public were not content to leave the Unit Minor in road-going trim, and very soon stripped examples were beginning to make their presence felt in the trials awards lists. Bob Foster, for one, employing trials as a winter relaxation from road racing, gathered quite a useful armful of silverware. In the Midlands, Len Vale-Onslow had several successes – notwithstanding the fact that he was a rival manufacturer, building the sporty SOS range.

Even more surprising was the enterprise of Dorking dealer, H. R. Nash, who sleeved a Unit Minor down to 123 cc, encased the lower part of the engine and the steering head in beaten-aluminium fairings, and added a streamlined tail of the same metal. At Brooklands in 1933 it won three out of its five races and lapped at 72·81 mph.

Greater glory was to come when, in May, 1934, Harry Nash wheeled out the diminutive New Imperial once more to take the five-kilometre and five-mile flying start, the ten-kilometre standing start, and ten-mile standing start world records, at speeds of up to 63·79 mph. And the beauty of the whole thing was that, apart from the cylinder sleeving and the use of streamlining, the bike was a perfectly standard roadster which Nash had taken from a customer in part-exchange for 'something a bit quicker'. It is nice to know, too, that the record-breaking New Imperial still exists, and in recent times has paid a nostalgic trip back to Brooklands, at Brooklands Society gatherings.

THE ROLLS-ROYCE OF MOTOR CYCLES

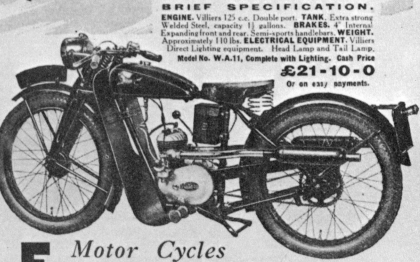
30

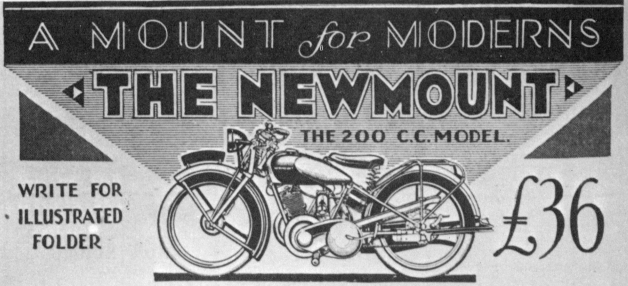
31

Bargains all the way

The year 1931 had been a flop season; 1932 could be written-off as disastrous. Even though every British manufacturer pared his prices to the bone, registrations continued down the slippery slope – in direct contrast to Germany and Italy, where there were more motor cyclists than ever before. One minor bright spot was the continued use by the Post Office of motor cycles for such purposes as telephone-line maintenance, and the collection and delivery of mail in remote areas. The placing of an order for 100 new commercial sidecar outfits for line work brought the total in use to well over 2,000.

A new National Government had come into power, with Neville Chamberlain as Chancellor of the Exchequer, and his 1932 budget speech furthered the scheme of taxation by cubic capacity. From June, 1933, a three-tier scale would be in force, with under-150 cc solos taxed at 15s (75p) as before, up-

to-250s at £1 10s (£1·50p), and over-250s at £3. The 224 lb weight limit was abandoned.

If anything, this favoured the 250 cc class at the expense of the popular 350 cc models (which now had to pay the same rate as big vee-twin Brough-Superiors, etc) and so the makers put in hand new two-fifties to meet the expected demand. That, though, was for next year, and meantime the slump went on.

It was indicative of the state of the market that the big dealers were already advertising clearance sales of brand-new stock as early as September, 1932. Pride and Clarke listed (among many other makes and models) the 349 cc BSA Blue Star, with tuned engine, high-level exhausts, and foot-change gearbox, at £38 12s 6d (£38·62½p) instead of the catalogue price of £45 5s (£45·25p); or you could have the super-sporty Sunbeam 492 cc Model 90, again with foot-change gearbox and guaranteed to reach 100 mph, reduced from £90 to £75.

Lovetts offered to supply any model from the Raleigh range at pounds below list price; Godfreys had Rudges at bargain rates; Laytons of Oxford tempted the customer with cut-price Francis-Barnetts, OK Supremes, Royal Enfields, and Wolves. Other main dealers offering large price reductions were Comerfords of Thames Ditton and Colmore Depot of Birmingham.

One particular machine was to emerge from this price-slashing melee as representative of the blackest days of the depression – the 250 cc Red Panther. The start of the story was an attractive new 250 cc single, the Phelon and Moore Model 40 Panther, designed by Frank Leach and introduced as one of the highlights of the 1932 Panther programme. Unlike the bigger Panthers, the little two-fifty employed a conventional front-down-tube frame within which to house the inclined-cylinder engine. Following Panther tradition, an oil compartment was incorporated in the crankcase castings.

On moving from Ariel to Triumph in 1932, Val Page redesigned the Coventry-built range and introduced the first semi-unit-construction Triumph 650 cc vertical twin, the 1933 Model 6/1. The gearbox bolted directly to the facing at the rear of the crankcase

Introducing
The NEW
BELSTAFF
"JUNIOR" STORM COAT

——— *embodying the practical suggestions of well-known riders and offered at a record low price.*

Proofed in such a way that rain runs off it like water off a duck's back. Every point in this wonderful new coat has been carefully studied, not only by the manufacturers, but also by some of the best-known riders in the country.   Note these great features :—

Be absolutely certain that the above label is sewn into the coat. Without it the coat cannot be a genuine Belstaff JUNIOR Storm Coat.

(1) Made of Finest Egyptian Super Gabardine (Fawn).

(2) Interlined with Belstaff Special Double "eggshell" Oilskin, BOTH sides treated.

(3) Lined with Pure Woollen Fleece.

(4) Cosy Detachable Pure Wool Neckscarf.

(5) New Quick-Swivel Fastening Grips at knees to prevent coat ends flapping open.

(6) Capacious Suede Cloth Pockets. Leather Cuffs.

PURE WOOLLEN FLEECE LINING
OILSKIN TREATED BOTH SIDES
FINEST EGYPTIAN GABARDINE

37'6

WITH

DETACHABLE PURE WOOL NECKSCARF

This most useful addition to the Belstaff JUNIOR Storm Coat is attached to the neck of the coat by two press buttons and fastens by buttons in front (see small sketch above). Extremely cosy, but instantly detachable when not required.

FREE GIFT

A SPECIAL SAFETY BELT FOR NIGHT RIDING is given Free with every Belstaff Junior Storm Coat. This is a tubular White Belt which you slip over the ordinary belt at the back, and it enables other motorists to see you at a great distance.

OTHER FAMOUS BELSTAFF COATS

The BELSTAFF SENIOR T.T. COMPETITION COAT made of supple non-cracking, non-peeling Black rubber-cloth. Complete with Saddle & Tummy Protector and Special Knee Fastener Grips

29'9
With Fleece Lining 7/6 extra.

The BELSTAFF SENIOR STORM COAT made of Dark Fawn finest Egyptian Gabardine in R.A.F. Style, oilskin interlined and fleece-lined throughout. Complete with Saddle and Tummy Protector - - - **45'-**

TWO YEARS GUARANTEE

With every Belstaff JUNIOR Storm Coat, the Manufacturers give a Two Years' Guarantee of Satisfaction or Free Replacement.   Go to your dealer at once and ask to see this amazing new coat !

If unobtainable locally, write us for address of nearest Stockist.

The BELSTAFF MFG. Co. Ltd.
Longton, Stoke-on-Trent

To the Trade: We do not supply the public direct, we leave this to you. Write for full details.

33

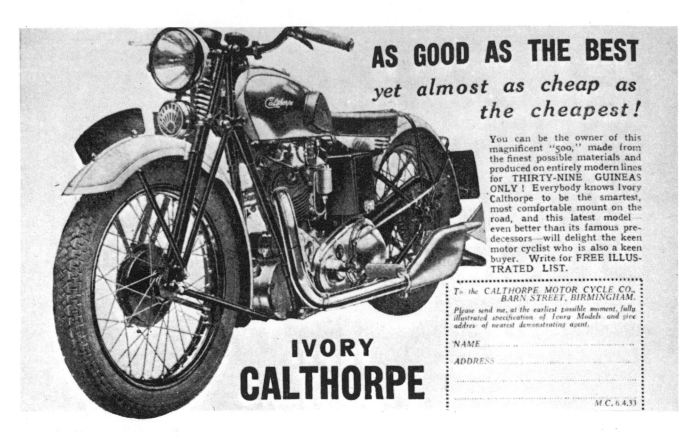

List price of the Model 40 was £42 10s (£42·50p), and at that the customer got Maglita electrics, about which an explanation would not be amiss at this point. The Maglita was a peculiar instrument which was driven at engine speed, and embodied both magneto and dynamo windings on the same armature. Engine speed was necessary, in order to generate sufficient current for the lights, but this meant, also, that the magneto part of the unit delivered a spark each time the piston came to the top of its stroke, whether this be the firing stroke or not. But should the ignition timing be less than spot on, there was a chance that the idle spark could cause a blow back through the carburettor – then up in flames would go the bike. It did indeed happen, on several occasions; not only with Panthers but with Rudges which also used Maglita equipment.

The tail end of the season saw Pride and Clarke disposing of unsold Model 40 Panthers, now labelled Red Panthers, at the unbelievable price of £28 10s (£28·50p). Understandably, they went like hot cakes, and soon Pride and Clarke were knocking on Phelon and Moore's door asking for more. Well, desperate times breed desperate measures, and up at Cleckheaton (which is in the Yorkshire woollen district) times were desperate indeed.

A deal was worked out whereby Phelon and Moore would produce, exclusively for Pride and Clarke, a 1933 250 cc Red Panther to sell, all in, at £28 17s 6d (£28·87½p). It would bring the Cleckheaton works no profit whatever, and the only advantage to the makers was that it would keep the works occupied. All the advertising and marketing would be Pride and Clarke's responsibility, leaving Panther with the job of just building the things.

In essence, it was much the same kind of deal under which present-day supermarket chains sell 'own label' products at prices below those of nationally-advertised lines, but the fantastically low price was only possible because the wool trade was in even worse plight that the motor cycle industry, and Phelon and Moore were able to recruit out-of-work millgirls to assemble the Red Panther at minimum wages. In addition, hard bargaining with outside suppliers could knock a penny a gross from this item or that, while thinner metal for the mudguards or chain covers could save further halfpence. Yes, it was sweated labour, agreed director Peter Marians, but the works had no option if they were to survive at all.

The first Pride and Clarke advertisements for the 'Sensation of 1933' appeared in the first week of that year, advertising the 'improved 1933 250 cc Red Panther' at £28 17s 6d (£28·87½p) inclusive of tools, horn, and electric lighting, and with full manufacturer's guarantee.

Panther's bread-and-butter came from the ultra-cheap Red Panther models, but for those with a little more money to spend the same firm offered luxury versions such as this 1934 348 cc Model 80, with twin-port cylinder head, upswept exhaust pipes, foot-change gearbox, etc

'How can we offer such wonderful value?', they asked, in a headline, and they appended their own reply. 'We have made special contracts with Messrs Phelon and Moore, whereby this machine is manufactured for and sold exclusively by us, making it possible to fix a retail price at a far lower figure than would otherwise have been practicable.'

In addition to the standard model, Pride and Clarke could supply a 250 cc Red Panther de luxe for £33 10s (£33·50p), the extra cost covering provision of Miller direct-current generator (dynamo) and coil ignition, and a larger headlamp. So far so good, but for 1934 the Red Panther afforded even greater value. True, the cost had gone up to £29 17s 6d (£29·87½p), the figure at which it will always be remembered, but that now included the Miller electrics. There was still a Red Panther de Luxe at £33 10s (£33·50p), and the additional cost now covered a four- instead of three-speed gearbox, an electric instead of bulb horn – and the licence holder was thrown in free, instead of being listed as an extra.

Through all of this and right up to 1939 the Red Panther was to have a higher-priced counterpart, available through other dealers. This was the Model 70, which for 1934 was priced at £41 15s (£41·75p). For economic reasons, the Red Panther and Model 70 used a large number of common parts, but for his

extra cash the Model 70 fancier had a twin-port cylinder head with twin upswept exhaust pipes, a cast-light-alloy oilbath primary chaincase instead of a pressed-steel cover, and a four-speed gearbox.

Down the years the bargain bike grew to maturity, reflecting always the progressive development of the higher-priced version. A more sophisticated rocker gear was adopted, with total enclosure of the valves and springs. A foot-change gearbox was specified at 10s (50p) extra. For a further 10s (50p) the customer could have a chromium-plated fuel tank with cream side panels.

Rock-bottom cheapie it certainly was, but the Red Panther was to prove totally reliable and tolerant of neglect. Primarily it was the factory employee's ride-to-work hack, with all that the term implies. Garaged in a back yard with no more protection than an old sack, fed on the cheapest possible fuel and oil, it was expected to keep going, come what may. And keep going was just what it did, with the thinly-applied chrome peeling from the tank and exhaust pipe, the rattling mudguards tied up with copper wire, and the crankcase coated with a thick goo of oil and road dirt.

Remarkably, the £29 17s 6d (£29·87½p) Red Panther was to be on offer right up to the week before the Second World War broke out. It was missing from the proposed 1940 Phelon and Moore catalogue; only then could we be sure that the days of the Depression were at last over.

To prove its toughness, a standard Red Panther was put through a series of tests at Brooklands under the eagle eye of an ACU observer. There was a consumption test, during which it covered 115·7

miles on a measured gallon at an average speed of 35·5 mph, a flying quarter-mile accomplished at 63·38 mph, a number of two-up stop-and-restart climbs on the 1-in-4 Brooklands Test Hill, and a timed extraction of the rear wheel (it took 1 minute 16 sec). Emerging with flying colours, the bike was awarded the coveted Maudes Trophy for 1933. One Red Panther even tackled the rigours of an Italian-based International Six Days Trial, in the hands of Ken Norris.

Cheap and cheerful, the 250 cc Red Panther (and there was a 350 cc model too, selling at about £35) was ridden and ridden until it dropped to pieces, and it is for that reason that so few have lasted to the present time. Initially, it was sold for peanuts; second-hand, it had negligible monetary value, and so countless clapped-out Red Panthers went for salvage. Only now can we stand back and appreciate just what extraordinary value for money it really was.

Mention of upswept (or high-level) exhaust pipes, and two-port cylinder heads may cause an eyebrow or two to lift, but that was the way fashion ran in the 1930s. The high-level exhaust came from the trials world, of course, where it served the very practical purpose of keeping the exhaust discharge above water level in deep splashes. But very soon road-going bikes were being equipped with high pipes, too, for no other reason than that they *looked*

sporty; this despite the anguished cries of female pillion riders, who suffered burnt legs and holed stockings in consequence.

Similarly, the two-port cylinder head, surmounting a single-cylinder engine, was of very dubious mechanical advantage, and for the most part served merely to give the machine a well-balanced appearance. There was a case to be made for twin pipes on a four-valve engine such as the Rudge, but on a two-valver it was just extra cost for the purchaser. In spite of that, as late as 1950 Ariel still offered the choice of single-port or twin-port heads on the Red Hunter models.

It was in 1933 that the slump hit bottom and, just perceptibly, began to bounce up again. The same year found another of the major British manufacturers – this time, Rudge – in severe trouble. Yet perversely it brought a brand-new make to the market; this was Majestic, a handsome machine available with 250, 350 or 500 cc ohv sloper engines, foot-change gearboxes and pleasantly rounded fuel tanks.

The Majestic was manufactured by Ernie Humphries, and although it emanated from the OK Supreme works at Bromley Street, Birmingham, Ernie insisted that it was an entirely separate make. In fact it was an attempt to take OK Supreme up-market, and although the venture was relatively short-lived, it did bring back into the picture the firm of Stevens Brothers (Wolverhampton) Ltd.

The crash of AJS had left the Stevens family in possession of their old works at Retreat Street, Wolverhampton. Almost before Matchless, new owners of the name, had managed to get AJS back into production at the Woolwich works, Harry and

After the liquidation of the original AJS company, George and Harry Stevens re-started production in the old AJS works in Retreat Street, Wolverhampton. The AJS trade-mark had been bought by Matchless, and so the new name of 'Stevens' was employed for the new range, of which this 1937 500 cc ohv is typical. The megaphone silencer, with detachable baffle, was standard equipment

George Stevens were in business at Retreat Street. The first product was a commercial three-wheeler, the 5 cwt Stevens light van, and soon this was joined by a range of engines, looking extremely like AJS power units, marketed under an Ajax (the nearest they could get to Ajay without actually saying so!) name.

The likeness was so remarkable that the only possible answer was that Harry and George had bought back, from Matchless, a number of surplus-to-requirement AJS jigs and tools. Failure of the Majestic encouraged the Stevens Brothers to go back into motor cycle manufacture on their own account. The bike was the Stevens, at first made in 250 cc form only, but later supplemented by 350 and 500 cc models. It deserves mention, if only for the fact that it introduced the megaphone-type silencer (with internal baffle) to the roadster world.

Rudge was very largely a family concern, headed by John Vernon Pugh, and when John Pugh fell ill the company began to run into difficulties. Paradoxically these were partly due to Rudge's racing success in 1930 and 1931. Development of the racing four-valve engines had cost a packet and, in normal times, Rudge could expect to cover this by increased sales following the racing victories. These, however, were not normal times. The huge factory at Crow Lane, Coventry, tried to recuperate by going in for proprietary-engine manufacture under a Python label (there was even a four-valve 175 cc Python for the European market, although it was not taken up by a British manufacturer).

Such measures were not enough to keep the wolf from the door, and in March, 1933, Rudge's creditors appointed an official receiver. Now, this could have been the end but, fortunately, the receiver did his best to keep the company going. Naturally, he had to keep tight financial reins on everything, and that meant shutting the racing department (but the works bikes were given into the care of the Graham Walker Syndicate, comprising the former members of the Rudge team – Ernie Nott, Tyrell Smith, and Graham himself – and it was under this label that the machines were raced in 1933 and 1934).

Through the period of receivership, Rudge roadsters continued to develop. They adopted left-side foot-change for the gearbox, and totally enclosed valve gear; first fitted to the official British ISDT Vase B models, a quickly-detachable rear wheel passed into standard production.

John Pugh died in 1936, and the official receiver was successful in finding a buyer for the now-viable company. New owners were the His Master's Voice radio and records combine now known as EMI, and during 1938 Rudge production was gradually transferred from Coventry to the HMV plant at Hayes, Middlesex. Rudge looked set for a happy future, and HMV sanctioned work on a 350 cc overhead-camshaft engine for future production. Also, they produced a 250 cc two-valver for prospective military use, and this was given the War Office go-ahead.

But only 200 of the British Army Rudges had been built when the entire HMV complex was requisitioned for the production of wartime radio and electronic equipment. So died the Rudge.

In 1933 there was evidence that the motor cycle makers, anyway, were sure that better things were under way at last in the introduction, by Triumph, of Britain's first production vertical twin. From the drawing board of Val Page (who had transferred from Ariel when that firm was shedding staff the year previously) this was a 650 cc semi-unit job, the gearbox being bolted directly to a machined facing at the rear of the crankcase; primary drive was by double-helical gearing.

Soundly constructed, but rather heavy in appearance, the Triumph twin was mainly intended for sidecar haulage (one feature was a ratchet by which the rear brake could be locked on, should there be need to park the outfit on a slope) and, accordingly, super-showman Harry Perrey – now with Triumph – gave it an introductory outing in the Scarborough Rally, following that with an appearance in the ACU's first-ever National Rally.

In this, the original intention had been a massive rally of ACU clubmen from all over Britain, meeting – at Eastbourne, it was suggested – for a day of fun and games, with trophies galore to take home. Somehow, though, it all went off at half-cock. The eventual meeting point turned out to be Barnet Grass Speedway, a dusty grass-track meadow alongside the Barnet By-Pass. More spectators than competitors turned up, and the whole thing was a ghastly mistake.

However, the ACU made a determined effort to do better the following year, when the finishing point was switched to Donington Park. This time there was more emphasis on the mileage competition, the event was a roaring success, and the National Rally became a permanent date in the keen clubman's diary – until the recent fuel crises, that is.

We have not yet done with 1933, because this proved to be the turning point in the sport of speedway, with the establishment of a Speedway Control Board, allied to the ACU. The cinders game is another story of the 1930s.

Flying cinders

Imported from Australia, speedway was a child of the late 1920s, but it was in the 1930s that it grew up and achieved recognition as a major sport. The first stirrings were seen in Britain early in 1928. Soon dirt-tracking had become a craze, with tracks springing up on any suitable (and often unsuitable) site. Good spectator facilities – crowd banking, grandstands, refreshments and toilet blocks – were a necessity, and for that reason many of the new venues were existing greyhound or football grounds. A few, however, were constructed especially for the cinders game, among them Owlerton (Sheffield), Brandon (Coventry), and Belle Vue (Manchester) – the present stadium, because early Belle Vue meetings were held at the greyhound track nearby. Regrettably, a few of the specially-laid tracks failed to survive for long; Greet Motordrome, Birmingham, failed after just two meetings.

Initially, a speedway programme was a hotchpotch of heats and finals, scratch and handicap events, match races, and demonstration rides by visiting stars. But the more astute promoters realised that the public, fascinated as they might be at the moment, would not be content for ever with the circus-style entertainment. A new approach was needed, something which would ensure that the fans would keep the turnstiles clicking merrily, week after week.

The answer was inter-track team racing, something with which local crowds could identify in the same way that football fans cheered on their teams come hell or high water. Gingerly at first, a Southern League got under way in mid-1929, followed by a corresponding Northern League. At first teams were of four men only. A match would be decided over nine heats, with the remainder of the evening filled in, as before, with track championships, races for the Silver Sash or Golden Gauntlet, and so on. Match points were reckoned on the basis of four points for a win, two for second place, and one for third.

It was a start, at least, and when the Southern League expanded their teams to six men (although the Northerners stuck to the original four-man concept) the crowds had still more reason to cheer on their heroes. The adoption of body colours –

overjackets bearing the symbol and colours of the different teams – improved the image even more.

It has to be said, however, that the Northern tracks, especially, were on none too sound a footing, and several of them were unable to complete their 1929 fixtures. Nevertheless, the 1930 season began with a Northern League comprising Belle Vue, Manchester White City, Preston, Liverpool, Sheffield, Warrington, Edinburgh, Barnsley, Leicester Super, Rochdale, Glasgow, Wombwell, and Newcastle Gosforth, with a number of these promotions loosely gathered under the banner of the Northern Track Owners Association.

The Southern League was made up of Wimbledon, Wembley, Southampton, Coventry, Stamford Bridge, Birmingham Hall Green, Lea Bridge, Crystal Palace, West Ham, Leicester Blackbird Road, Harringay, Kings Oak, and Nottingham. In addition, at least another half-dozen tracks, including Birmingham Perry Barr, Exeter, Portsmouth,

One of the early British speedway stars, Les Blakeborough, had the bright idea in 1931 of staging speedway on *concrete* instead of cinders. To permit the bike to broadside the corners, he equipped a rear wheel of his Wallis-Blackburne with balls on angled pivots instead of a tyre. The idea worked, but not convincingly enough, and was never taken up

First British speedway to stage night-time racing under floodlights was Stamford Bridge, where the track was around the Chelsea football pitch. Its main drawback was the narrowness of the track, which made passing difficult. A popular Stamford Bridge teamster was Dicky Smythe, seen with his short wheelbase, four-valve Rudge in 1932

Halifax, and Salford were licenced, but outside the league structure; these carried on with friendly matches, and the various other types of competition – two-lap dashes, individual track-record attempts, and so on – that had been popular in the previous two seasons.

Promotion was largely in the hands of professional companies like International Speedways Ltd, and Dirt-Track Speedways Ltd, but because this was motor cycle sport, of a kind, the ruling body was the Auto-Cycle Union. And it was the ACU which introduced, from January, 1930, an official contract form which had to be signed by both parties whenever a promoter engaged a rider. It was, in the ACU spokesman's own words, 'in every way a thoroughly legal document which contains absolutely no loopholes, leaks, or other undesirable exits through which a promoter – or a rider – can wriggle.'

From the same date, it was no longer necessary for a speedway rider to be in possession of an open ACU competition licence (which allowed him to compete, if he so wished, in events such as the TT races and the Scottish Six Days Trial) and, instead, a special speedways-only licence costing a guinea (£1·05p) a year was introduced.

A further ACU edict was to the effect that for the 1930 season and onwards *they* would conduct the league, not the promoters associations (which, in any case, were frequently warring with each other).

As racing got under way, it became clear that although most of the Southern tracks were settling down nicely, all was far from well with the maverick Northerners. Barnsley was the first to close, in July, falling attendances being quoted as the reason. Sheffield's Saturday evening meetings were cancelled because it was becoming difficult to attract 'star status' riders (who were paid more than the rank and file). In the far South-West, the Exeter County Ground track was closed pending an appeal against an injunction obtained by a local resident on the score of excessive noise.

Like many another, Liverpool operated at a greyhound stadium, and promoter Ossie Wade (a former TT rider) eyed the totalisator facilities at the venue and made formal application for an experimental meeting to be run with the tote in operation. That was turned down by the ACU, who felt that the introduction of betting at a motor cycle race meeting of any kind could lead to bribery, corruption, nobbling, and who-knows-what! But at least Ossie had asked.

Meanwhile there had been trouble at Audenshaw, a horse-trotting track in South Manchester which had hosted some of the earliest speedway meetings seen in the North. In 1930 it was not only outside the league, but had no ACU licence, yet on Sunday,

June 29, a group of former South Manchester MCC officials staged an unlicenced meeting at which the competitors wore face masks – not to protect themselves from flying cinders but to avoid recognition. The meeting had been well advertised, and more than 12,000 spectators had passed through the turnstiles when part of the outside fence was broken down – and a further 5,000 got in without paying. Such was the crush that a number of spectators crossed the track to stand on the centre green, and several accidents were avoided only by the greatest of good fortune. Naturally, the ACU set up a court of enquiry, and the outcome was that 12 registered riders had their licences revoked, another 22 who had no ACU licences were barred fom applying for any, and nine officials were suspended.

There was, moreover, a sequel. The Rochdale promotion was in a rocky financial state, and in early August it announced that the track was about to close and the team would be unable to complete their fixtures. Yet a week or two later Rochdale was back in action, under new management. At one of the resumed meetings it was noted that four bookmakers had set up their stalls and were raking in the punters' money. Again an ACU court of enquiry was instituted, when it was discovered that Rochdale's 'new management' was, in fact, our old friends from banned Audenshaw. So eleven more riders and officials were suspended.

But for all the shenanigans up North, speedway was about to enter happier times with the inauguration of a series of test matches between teams representing England and Australia. In a sense, this was akin to a Former Pupils v Masters tournament, because the Australians had brought the game to Britain in the first place, and it was they who had shown budding native stars how the loose-surfaced tracks should be ridden.

A five-match series was planned, with the first meeting on 30 June at Wimbledon, followed by Belle Vue on 23 July, Stamford Bridge on 20 August, Sheffield on 3 September and (well, but of course!) a grand finale at Wembley on 26 September. For the first four matches the teams would be six a side, but for Wembley's big night the teams would be increased to eight men apiece, with the match running to 16 heats.

For the record, Vic Huxley was appointed Australian captain, and his squad for the Wimbledon opener comprised Frank Arthur, Billy Lamont, Ron Johnson, Max Grosskreutz, and Dicky Case. Captained by 'Smiling Jim' Kempster (a former HRD works road-tester, who was to lose his life late in the Second World War when his plane crashed over northern Germany), the England team was formed of Frank Varey, Roger Frogley, Jack Parker, Wal Phillips, and Jack Ormston (now a well-known racehorse trainer).

Described by the contemporary press as 'certainly the best show Wimbledon has ever staged', the meeting attracted a packed house, with the start delayed by half an hour to allow would-be spectators to jam in. Even at that, several thousand more had to stand outside and listen to the cheers.

Four times, Vic Huxley beat the track record, finally leaving it at 72·6 sec. With points scoring now on a 3-2-1 basis, Australia won the night by 35 points to 17 (several heats had only two finishers, through falls and machine troubles) and, indeed, were to go on to win the series. But it is worth while casting a glance at the Wembley final.

For their eight-man squad, the Aussies dropped Frank Arthur, and brought in Bluey Wilkinson, Charlie Spinks, and Jack Chapman. England, however, had a much-changed side, now captained by Roger Frogley, with backing from Ormston, Parker, Varey, Gus Kuhn, Squib Burton, Frank Charles, and Colin Watson.

Unhappily, it rained, and continued to bucket down throughout the evening, leaving big pools on the track, yet 25,000 fans paid to come in, and so the Wembley management – who had planned introductory parades, cheer-leaders and all the other bally-hoo of which the stadium is so famous – decided to cut out the preliminaries and get straight down to business. Machines were sliding all over the place, riders falling off left, right and centre; but it was a cracking match, in spite of it all, with England gaining the upper hand in Heat 11 and running out winners on the night at 49 points to 45.

So far, the bugbear of speedway (and a polite press despatch from the ACU early in 1931 asked newspapers and other journals to refer to the sport by that name and not by the rather derogatory term of 'dirt track') had been in the starting system. Many bikes, notably the long-wheelbase Douglas flat twins, were not equipped with clutches and so a rolling start was instigated. This meant that the riders circled the track slowly, trying their best to be four-abreast as they came up to the starting line; if they managed it, the starter switched on a green light, and the race was on. But a four-abreast line was not easy to maintain, and frequently there would be a couple of false starts before a race started in earnest. As can be imagined, all this caused spectators to lose interest, and obviously a better system had to be devised.

From Easter, 1933, the newly-appointed Speed-

West Ham's 1938 squad, captained by the legendary Bluey
Wilkinson (standing, with hand on the bars of the miniature
bike). The mascot is young Ian Hoskins, currently
promoting speedway at Newcastle-Upon-Tyne, and behind
him is the even-more-legendary Johnny Hoskins, the
showman who brought speedway to Britain in 1928 and, in his
late 80s, was still involved with the sport at Canterbury

way Control Board insisted that starts would
henceforth be by clutch, with engines running.
Although the ruling had caused some prior apprehension among riders, it worked reasonably well, the
start signal being given by flag. There were still some
false starts, however, and it was evident that riders
needed to be faced with a physical barrier until the
moment the race started – something like the rising
tapes used at horse-race meetings, for example.

Joint promoters at Crystal Palace (and at Exeter
and Birmingham Perry Barr, for that matter) Fred
Mockford and Cecil Smith came up with a 'gate' –
tapes stretching across the track which would whip
up and away, by means of elastic, when the starter
pulled a lever to release the catches. It was tried out,
gingerly, during the second half of a Crystal Palace
meeting in June, and although the action was at first
too slow, stronger elastic cured the problem, and a
week later the Control Board gave the OK for it to
be standardised for all league racing.

Not that the tape gate cured all the troubles at
once, because very soon the craftier types were

watching the starter's hand rather than the tapes,
and as soon as the lever began to move, they were
away. Electro-magnetic gate catches, released by a
starter out of sight of the riders, settled that (in fact,
such gates are employed to this day).

With the weaker tracks weeded out, speedway
settled down to one combined National League,
although in 1934 a Second Division was established,
initially with teams of reserves from First Division
Belle Vue, Harringay, Wembley, Perry Barr, and
New Cross. The Second Division was a useful
adjunct, serving to bring on novices, provide
veterans with not-too-strenuous exercise, and
acclimatise newly-arrived Australians – and Americans, too, for by 1934 speedway had caught on in a
big way across the Atlantic, with no fewer than 12
tracks operating in California.

There had been Americans on British tracks in the
earliest days, men such as Sprouts Elder and Art
Pecher, but as the 1930s ran on so a second wave
arrived, including Jack and Cordy Milne, and
Wilbur Lamoreaux, and their calibre was such that
Jack Milne was winner of the 1937 World Speedway
Championhip, with Lammy Lamoreaux in runner-
up spot, and Cordy Milne third.

The previous year, the first World Individual
Riders' Championship Final, recognised as such by
the FICM (the international governing body of
motor cycle sport), was run off before an ecstatic

Above: speedway action, 1939 style, as England get to grips with Australia at New Cross Stadium (off Old Kent Road, London) in the first Test Match of the season. Taking a wide line is England captain Arthur Atkinson, while Aussie captain Lionel van Praag hugs the inside, and Charlie Spinks brings up the rear. England won, by 62 to 46 points

Right: America's contribution to the establishment of speedway is often overlooked, but early stars like Art Pechar and Sprouts Elder should never be forgotten. In the later 1930s, brothers Jack and Cordy Milne made a considerable impact (they are seen in a 1936 shot), with Jack, in 1937, becoming the first USA rider to take the World Speedway Championship title

75,000 crowd at Wembley, and it is illuminating to glance back at the way in which the competition was organised.

There had originally been a selected entry of 63 riders, who took part in a preliminary round in which nine of the entry were allocated to each of seven tracks. The four highest scorers from each of the seven meetings were brought together, so that there were 28 men to battle through the second round. This time each of the seven chosen tracks staged a 20-heat meeting, to which 16 of the qualifiers were allocated. This meant that each rider visited four tracks and, eventually, rode against every other qualifier.

From that round, the 16 top scorers won through to the Wembley final. In addition, however, the qualifiers were awarded bonus points based on their percentage performances in the qualifying rounds so, for the record, the finalists, with their bonus points, were: Eric Langton, 13; Frank Charles, George Newton, Jack Parker, and Lionel van Praag, all 12; Morian Hansen, Bob Harrison, Vic Huxley,

and Bluey Wilkinson, all 10; Dicky Case, Jack Ormston, and Jack and Cordy Milne, all 9; and Ginger Lees, Wal Phillips, and Joe Abbott, all 7.

Through injuries received prior to Wembley, Joe Abbott and Jack Parker were non-starters, and so the next highest scorers in the qualifiers, Arthur Atkinson and Bill Pitcher, rode as substitutes.

Right from the start, the crowd was kept on tiptoe, with Charles snatching victory in the first heat from Case and Phillips, at the same time knocking 1·4 sec off the Wembley track record. Even so, it was not to be Frank Charles's night. He kept his unbeaten score as far as Heat 9, but then his machine reared as the tapes went up, van Praag gated well and shot away in the lead, and from then on Charles slipped back down the ladder.

Not until Heat 20, the last on the programme, did the two heroes of the night – Lionel van Praag and Eric Langton – meet each other. Eric was on 24 points, Lionel on 23, and once the gate shot up it was a dog-fight all the way. Eventually van Praag crossed the line, winner by less than a machine's

length, and that brought both men level on 26 points.

A run-off was therefore necessary, and again the two were locked in battle for the full distance, with van Praag gaining the title, the trophy, and a £500 cheque by inches only, while Eric had to be content with £250. In third place came Bluey Wilkinson (West Ham and Australia), which was tough luck for him, because on final night he was unbeaten, and his lower placing was the result of amassing fewer bonus points in the qualifying rounds.

Still, Bluey (actual name was Arthur, but nobody called him that) was to have his day two years later, when he took the title ahead of Jack Milne and Wilbur Lamoreaux – and the 1936 champion, Lionel van Praag, was way down in fourth spot.

There never was a 1939 World Championship final, although Wembley had gone ahead with stadium alterations, to accommodate an anticipated record 100,000 crowd. The meeting should have been held in September, of course; except that a certain Adolf Hitler precipitated an even more international clash . . .

So it was that pre-war big-time speedway came to an end in the last week of August, 1939 (although Belle Vue, alone, carried on with a series of scratch meetings until peace returned), with the staging, at Wembley, of the fifth and final England v Australia test match of the year. The fact that England gave the Aussies a terrific drubbing, by 71 points to 36, was beside the point. What really counted was that two newcomers to the England side – Tommy Price and Malcolm Craven – together scored 20 of England's 71 point total, while the Australians produced, in Vic Duggan, a man who was widely tipped as the potential 1939 World Champion. Whether Vic could indeed have taken the title, we shall now never know.

Below: the instant popularity of the new sport of speedway led many British manufacturers to produce special machines for the job. However, the one which offered the biggest threat to the all-conquering Douglas was the short-wheelbase Rudge four-valve. Although it dictated a less spectacular riding style, it got round the bends quicker, and that was what counted!

Bottom: king of the tracks in the early years of speedway was the long and low Douglas, which demanded a leg-trailing riding style, and cornering which threw up a wave of black cinders. But after several seasons at the top of the heap it was overthrown by the Rudge, which in turn had to give best to the JAP

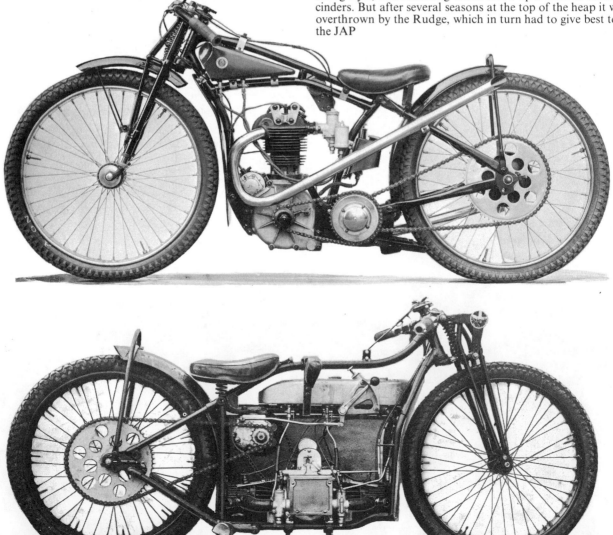

As the decade began, the snarling Douglas twin was undoubted king of the tracks, cornering in spectacular broadsides with the rider trailing his steel-toecapped left boot in the cinders and spraying the trackside crowds. But spectacle is one thing, and it is not necessarily the quickest way round a speedway track, so by 1930 the Douglas had a fight on its hands, with the main opposition coming at first from the four-valve Rudge, a short-wheelbase machine campaigned by Jim Kempster, Billy Lamont, and other top-liners.

At the 1929 London Show, however, Bill Bragg paid a visit to the JAP stand, and there tackled Vivien Prestwich and designer Stan Greening on the possibility of building a JAP speedway engine. The JAP folk agreed, and by March, 1930 the first speedway JAP engine was in being. Frankly, it was a lash-up, with the crankcase of the firm's 350 cc road racer, the cylinder barrel of their 500 cc racer but with the fins cropped, and the whole was topped by a 350 cc roadster head. It weighed only 37 lb.

Soon, a production model was under way, with an extremely wide power band and producing, on alcohol, 33 bhp at anything up to 6,000 rpm. Four engines were made, and were passed out to Bragg, and to Vic Huxley, Frank Arthur, and Billy Lamont. At first, the track performance was disappointing, the engine proving no match for the Rudge four-valver, but a new inlet cam and a larger inlet valve pushed the bhp output up a couple of notches.

One of the most famous machines of the 1928-33 period was the Harley-JAP ridden by England skipper Colin Watson. Frame and front forks are those of a 350 cc Harley-Davidson Peashooter; the present engine, replacing the original JAP, was fitted by Colin in 1931. Restored by Mike Lawrence, the bike has been exhibited at a number of recent speedway meetings

Wal Phillips was the first to try the redesigned engine, and he took to it immediately, to such good effect that he gained 14 successive victories. Another JAP engine was installed in the Harley frame of Wembley Lions captain, Colin Watson, and with this hybrid model (still existing, in the ownership of Vintage MCC member, Mike Lawrence) he set a new national quarter-mile record, and took track records at Wimbledon and Crystal Palace.

Douglas were not yet done, and the factory fought back with a revised flat-twin (equipped with clutch), but after three years of struggle the single won the day. With the advent of the foot-forward style of riding, JAP victory was total, and was to remain so right through to the coming of the Jawa in post-war times.

America, too, took to the JAP, much to the chagrin of the Harley-Davidson factory. After all, their Peashooter single had been prominent at the start of speedway, and now Harleys came forward with an entirely new speedway machine, of very 'British' appearance. This was unveiled by Walter and Bill Davidson in person at the 1934 New York Show, and *Motorcyclist*, the American monthly magazine, declared it to be 'The most racing sickle that 465 bucks ever bought'.

So closely had the Harley-Davidson folk copied European practice that the new engine was directly interchangeable with the JAP speedway motor, so allowing American riders the opportunity of 'Harley-Davidson powerising of present equipment'. Soon another USA-built competitor had come on the scene, in the shape of the Crocker, but any success gained by either make was of only local significance. World-wide, the JAP ruled speedway, and that was all there was to it.

The wit and wisdom of 'Ixion'

No motor cyclist, in the whole history of the movement, has ever been held in such high esteem, or regarded with such genuine affection, as 'Ixion', whose weekly pages enlivened the pages of *The Motor Cycle* right through from the 1900s to his death in 1962. Who was 'Ixion'? In his lifetime the secret was closely guarded, and not until his pen had been stilled for ever was it revealed that in fact he had been Canon Basil H. Davies.

Throughout the 1930s, readers looked forward eagerly to their weekly ration of wit and wisdom, and whatever the current topic, 'Ixion' was sure to have some appropriate comment to make. Frequently, too, his 'Occasional Comments' pages would be illuminated by a pen-and-ink sketch from Sydney Raphael Jones, who himself had been contributing to *The Motor Cycle* from the earliest days. Paragraphs and sketches complemented each other marvellously, so in this section the artist and the writer have been brought together again, to provide for a younger generation, just a little of the flavour of those chuckling pages so enjoyed by your fathers and grandfathers.

First, though, in 'Ixion's' own words, the explanation of why Basil Davies adopted his famous nom-de-plume and, equally important, just how he liked the name to be pronounced.

WHEN one of the Editor's predecessors offered me a job on the staff of the 'Blue 'Un'* way back in the long ago, I had just got smashed up on my stinkwheel as the result of dividing my attention between the road and the fairy of the moment, whom, being still grass-green, I definitely worshipped as a goddess. So when I was told to find a pseudonym, as my managing director refused to sully his pages with my homely Lancashire patronymic of Murgatroyd, I naturally chose that of 'Ixion', a mythological person condemned by Jupiter to be broken on the wheel as a punishment for lifting amorous eyes to the queen of the classical heaven. I didn't forsee that most people would pronounce its first two syllables to rhyme with 'Dixie'; or that periodically they would quarrel with each other on the subject, and send me letters about it. For the umpteenth time, gentlemen, the second 'i' in my pseudonym is as *long* as you can make it, thus: 'Icks-*eye*-on'. The second 'i' is not only long, but is also the emphasised syllable. A good name, says the office boy, because I am always talking about myself.

28 July 1932

Although the next extract refers specifically to the under-150 cc machines which gained a tax concession in the 1931 budget of Philip Snowden, much of it could apply equally well today.

*The leading rival motor cycling journals of the period were the 'Blue 'Un' (*The Motor Cycle*) and the 'Green 'Un' (*Motor Cycling*).

A Norfolk scene on the coast road between Cromer and Wells, showing old Cley windmill

Staithes, Yorkshire

I WANT to return to the question of the retailer and the ultra-cheap lightweight. Most motor cycle dealers of the smaller type sell push-bikes, and they all tell me that they'd rather sell push-bikes than deliver a very cheap motor bike to a novice. The customer who buys a push-bike probably doesn't enter the shop again for a year, and when at last he reappears he wants a new cover or a brake bit, and expects to pay for it. But the novice who buys a cheap motor bike and returns a few days later may want anything imaginable, and doesn't expect to pay for it. He (or she) may even have forgotten to oil the engine, and may demand that the long-suffering unit, which he has welded-up solid, shall be restored to Brooklands tune at no charge. If the retailer consents he is heavily out of pocket; if he doesn't consent the customer stalks off in a towering rage, adopts another garage, and when he wins an Irish Sweep and buys a Rolls, the other garage snaffles the rake-off on the deal. That is why the agents

are not very keen on pushing Snowdens. I don't know any other trade in which a customer demands lots of free services. If I buy a suit of clothes I never worry the tailor afterwards, provided the suit is right at delivery. If it creases across the shoulders at once he naturally corrects the fit free of charge; but if I tear a trouser leg or spill my soup down my vest I pay for repairs. Retailers would leap at the chance of selling Snowdens by the thousand if they got a clear profit on the deal, however tiny the profit. Of course the real culprit is the weak trader, who lets awkward or greedy customers bully him and exploit him. The manufacturers might help by issuing with each machine a chart of official prices for various service jobs. Exactly the same trouble arose when very cheap cars were first launched; but the car retailer has now consolidated his position and displays no reluctance whatever to sell a £100 job. A similar firmness in the motor cycle retail world would soon set the Snowdens selling freely.

7 January 1932

Yes, there'll be quite a few heads nodding in sympathy with that one; and talking of sympathy, 'Ixion' had a word or two to say on the subject of the coming of motor cycle police in 1930.

THE Blue 'Un has some dear, thoughtful lads among those who go fagless and unbeered on Thursdays. For instance, one I will call Carnera jun., is worrying no end about these new speed cops whom Mr Morrison is setting to watch over us. Carnera Jun. wanted some waders for the winter, and all innocently selected a make which is built in France. Told his agent to order a pair. Agent took one increduluous glance at Carnera Jun.'s feet, and ordered the superest outsize. Superest

outsize arrived and on test seized-up on Carnera Jun.'s big toe. French factory asked for a pair of Carnera Jun.'s shoes to use as templates. Shoes sent. Great excitement in French factory. French *mécanicien* (super outsize) selected, and Canera Jun.'s shoes were at last jammed on his feet with aid of three kilos of cotton waste. Then a pair of waders was finally designed to fit. And now Carnera Jun. is worrying about the speed cops, who will have to scrap all over England on 100 mph ohv's in bitter winter weather, and probably won't be able to get waders till May, unless the Blue 'Un warns Mr Morrison here and now that contract and specifications should be put through at once. But, my dear Carnera Jun., your anxiety is totally unnecessary. An ordinary cop has to be large, so that he can master inebriated stevedores and the like. An ordinary cop has to stand on point duty for hours at a time, so that the kind of foot typical of a large, strong man necessarily becomes flattened in the course of thirty years' perpetually beating and pointing, or whatever they call it. But the *speed* cops won't have abnormal feet. Mr Morrison will

probably set a thief to catch a thief. He'll take the also-rans from our speed competitions – the men who just aren't good enough to win TT races and demand £2,000 a year from a factory, but are plenty fast enough to ride down you and me. They won't have any beating and pointing to do, and their feet will be normal. But you are a dear, thoughtful lad all the same.

2 October 1930

Any explanation needed to the above? Well, Herbert Morrison was Home Secretary at the time, and Primo Carnera, the 'Ambling Alp' was an enormous Italian who became world heavyweight boxing champion. But now, let us turn to another weighty subject. Until the Snowden budget of 1931, motor cycles could qualify for a £1 10s annual taxation rate, provided they weighed under 200 lb (raised to 224 lb from January, 1932) but the onus of providing a certificate of weight lay on the rider. Similarly, owners of present-day Reliant three-wheelers are sometimes asked to provide proof that their cars weigh less than 8 cwt, to avoid car tax, and that means a trip to a public weighbridge. They, especially, will appreciate the next comment.

The old packhorse bridge at Allerford, near Porlock, Somerset

MY barber was seccotining my few remaining locks to make the best show possible when I blew my nose. He detected a faint aroma of BP – yes, I'd stuffed my hankie in the air intake of the Sprint Special that morning to get an instantaneous start from cold. So Mr Barber regaled me during seccotining with the story of his attempts to licence his new motor bike. The catalogue weight was 210 lb, and he'd pushed it lightly on to the scales, much as a burglar regards a 'tec when he hasn't got a jemmy up the leg of his trousers. Suddenly – crash! – the scale indicator shot up to well over the fateful 224 lb, and stuck there! The next fifteen minutes produced a violent altercation, as the barber successively removed tools, spares, horn, and other fittings, and the County Council man reproachfully heaped all but the tools and spares back on the scales. Finally the barber departed, all hot, bothered and unlicensed. He is still musing whether he shall:

(1) Sue the manufacturer concerned;
(2) Reduce his wife's Saturday allotment and pay full tax;
(3) Be naughty and wheel the bike down to the weighbridge again, but this time minus flywheels, armature, and battery.

In this particular instance the manufacturer has apparently stated a weight for the standard model, and forgotten to add that dynamo equipment puts the bus outside the 30s tax. But purchasers, if they wish to economise in tax, should evidently be careful to verify weights of machines near the border line.

23 October 1930

Something of a camping fanatic, 'Ixion' would occasionally slip a country recipe into his column. This next one, in particular, became quite famous as the favourite supper dish of several star riders who spotted it in the Blue 'Un's pages. Maybe present-day readers would like to give it a try?

MANY readers weigh-in with advice about Jake's West Country dish, for which an angry North also claims domicile. The recipe runs: Procure one 1,000 cc Spanish onion. At the next stage doctors differ. Some say, 'Bisect and reassemble onion' (query; with Seccotine?). Others say, 'Cut cylindrical plug from north apex of onion' (query; with special die-stamping tool? *Why* do recipes always omit these vital details!) In cylindrical orifice thus created insert (a) large skinned kidney; (b) slice of tomato; (c) piece of butter the size of a headlamp bulb; (d) pepper; (e) salt. Replace piston in cylinder and insert assembly in pot. Half-submerge pot in water, adding a piece of dripping. Cover pot with a plate and place assembly in oven. Don't cook too slowly or too long. The heat should suffice to brown the outside of the onion nicely at the end of three hours.

Mrs Ixion hungrily and greedily awaits further information on how to reassemble the onion, if bisected; or, alternatively, what tool should be used to die-stamp cylindrical orifice in north pole of onion. She has asked me to grind a cutting edge on the lower skirt of the piston of my 150 cc two-stroke and has received an appropriate reply.

14 February 1935

An old house once the 'First and Last'
coaching inn, at Croscombe,
near Shepton Mallet, Somerset

Opposite: Stanton-in-the-Peak,
Derbyshire

But 'Ixion's' tips concerned other things besides cookery. Wrapped up in his whimsical word-imagery were some gems of road lore, and although the next hint would be difficult to apply today (car fuel tanks are rather less accessible) it may raise a reminiscent smile or two.

MY pal Stanley has large, wistful blue eyes. Always an asset in a world mostly populated by women, but not (one would think) of special value whilst motor cycling. But think again. Stanley ran out of petrol on the public road – a horrid business in these days of stern petrol tanks pumped by electric petrol lifts, and at times when all other motor cyclists seem to have deserted the road you're on.

So Stanley did his blue-eyed stuff on every car that came along with a woman at the wheel. Anon a lovely young creature stopped, and Stanley, concentrating all his blueness on her, begged permission to uncouple the car's petrol pipe. She surveyed him scornfully, and produced a bottle of Worthington from her picnic basket, 'Drink this!' she commanded.

Stanley, perplexed but wholly unloath, obeyed. She then looped a bit or wire around the neck of Mr Worthington, removed her enormous petrol-filler-cap, lowered Mr Worthington into the tank, and brought up one pint of Mr Pratt. (Author's note: Pratt's Motor Spirit became, in the mid-1930s, Esso or, as it is known in some parts of the world, Exxon.)

Stanley waxed positively oily in praise of

her resource and generosity. As she departed, the fairy snapped over her shoulder 'I've got a fool brother who is just as casual as you are. It's his tip.'

21 June 1934

Derived initially from signal lights pioneered by the Liverpool Overhead Railway, colour-light traffic signals (or 'robots') at cross roads had been in use for several years as the decade began. But by 1934, a fresh element had been added . . .

YOU all know Eva – the latest form of robot signal, actuated by contact strips in the roadway. Also, being motor cyclists, you relish an engineering discussion. Well, at a place where four cross-roads meet in the South of England there was an Eva. In the same place there were five motor cyclists. They coquetted with Eva. They found that if Eva was blushing (ie, showing red) and you rolled gently over the contact strip on your International Replica Panthudge, she'd turn bilious (amber) and also jealous (green) just before you arrived at the lamps.

So the quintette fell to discussing what would happen if four cars arrived simultaneous-like on all four contact strips. The discussion waxed a little heated and, finally, at 11 pm Alec led the gallant four to interview Eva.

They waited carefully till the beat policeman was well away round the corner. Then Alec assumed an Ebby-like posture in the dead centre of the crossroads with an arm upraised. The other four stationed themselves in an attitude of expectancy, one beside each contact strip. When Alec dropped his arm, each lad jumped heavily and firmly on to one of Eva's contact strips. What happened?

The answer is quite simple. When the four experimenters actuated the four strips simultaneously, two roads were getting the red and two the green. The problem is therefore just the same as if only two men or two vehicles are concerned – and the action is that described in a recent article in *The Motor Cycle*, viz., if two strips are depressed simultaneously, right of way is automatically given to the road which was getting the green at the moment of contact.

Ergo, even if four six-wheel lorries all sit on the contacts at the same moment, and stay there, the green lamps which are already

The Bell, Stilton, on the Great North Road

showing will continue to show unless the experimenters get bored, or a cop happens along!

19 April 1934

Each June, *The Motor Cycle* was wont to publish a stirring fictional tale, written by 'Ixion', in which some backroom inventor, or penniless hero, would devise a TT-winning machine. All good 'Boy's Own Paper' stuff, but I have more than a suspicion that the following paragraph (not from a TT number but from his regular weekly column) is not fiction at all.

THE factory was in the hands of a receiver. The managing director and financier-in-chief was in a nursing home, slowly convalescing after a serious operation. The brainy lad at the works evolved a design which promised to sidestep the trouble which had always snagged their machines in the TT. Receiver adamant. Not a copper! Not an hour of time! Not a pound of steel! Plausible lad from works sent with bunch of roses and some drawings to the nursing home. Much coaxing. Returns with cheque for £500. Engine built. Machine entered for TT. All done by unpaid overtime, receiver conceding nothing but use of tools. Week before TT, machine does 105 on quiet road at dawn. Next day engine melts. Plausible lad revisits nursing home with more roses. Returns with cheque for £250. Engine No. 2 (modified) sails for Island. Engine melts

in practice. Plausible lad revisits nursing home – gardenias this time. Engine No. 3 (further modified) reaches Island – finishes! The appropriate sequel should be that Engine No. 4 wins the 1934 TT. *Qui vivra, verra.* Meanwhile, do we who sit on hedges and grandstands ever realise what agonising hopes and struggles are transmuted into decibels on the Manx course each year?

31 August 1933

The factory was probably Rudge, the ailing managing director John V. Pugh, but more or less the same situation arose in 1936 at New Imperial. The absentee boss on this occasion was Norman T. Downs, who, paying a convalescent visit to the factory in early Spring, learnt that during his illness the remaining directors had voted not to support a racing programme. Downs was furious, immediately re-opened the racing shop, and the outcome was Bob Foster's 250 cc TT win, the last time a British-built machine ever won that race. But now for a few of 'Ixion's' recollections of pioneering times.

IN sob-stuff novels, films and plays the grey-haired mother weeps over a golden curl. The curl was once little Henry's. Little Henry is now big Henry and has just got three years for beating-up a policeman, or something of that sort. I grew quite sentimental yesterday over two weird objects which fell out of a small box consigned to me at Tudor Street. They were sparking plugs, vintage about 1900. There is one thing to be said in their favour – a London store used to retail such cheap plugs at 9d (4p) a time, but they were by no means as cheap as they looked. I have modern plugs listed at 5s (25p) or so which I bought two or three years ago, and have had in a variety of engines for many thousand miles. The prehistoric plugs seldom lasted 100 miles. They had porcelain insulators, slender as a Venus pencil, and electrodes little thicker than florists' wire. You couldn't take them to pieces, for the porcelain was cemented into the brass butt. The betting used to be evens on any of three untimely ends. Perhaps the body of the plug blew clean out and hit the underside of the tank with a resounding tang. Or else the insulator cracked across, and when you looked down you saw the plug doing a fox-trot in its socket. Or else one of the electrodes fell off and wandered about inside your engine. I used to buy them by the gross and use them by the dozen; one never thought of starting out with less than four spares for a single-cylinder engine, and I would carry a dozen on a London-Edinburgh ride.

25 December 1930

Plugs at 25p each? Not for the apprentice of 1934 or so, struggling to keep his 98 cc Excelsior Minor running, on a weekly wage of 7s 6d (37½p) a week. But Woolworths were still selling ex-RAF sparking plugs – exotic-looking things with cooling fins and mica insulators – at 6d (2½p) a time. There was an even cheaper alternative, because a visit to the local car-breaker's yard (which was something of a regular Saturday-afternoon ritual) would result in a pocketful of plugs – you borrowed the car-breaker's spanner and extracted them yourself from the engines piled up in one corner of the yard – at 1d (less than ½p) apiece. But for a final dip into Ixiondom, here are his comments on the blackout, as printed in the early days of the Second World War; a serious subject but, as always, his quirky humour shines through.

THE blackout has reminded the highbrows of ancient times when all streets were unlit, and peds had to provide their own illumination, as motorists do now. The most famous folk in those far-off days were apparently the gentlemen of Dursley, Glos, who when returning from a carouse used to pull the white tails of their shirts outside their trousers, so that they should not be rammed astern by post-chaises; thus the term 'Dursley Lantern' came into being. The notion is worthy of scientific consideration after the war. After dark no public or private illumination is orthochromatic. A cart, a bicycle, a drunken man, a turf edging – all look the same dun colour by the light of a headlamp. But even in the glare of a P100 white, praise be, is still white. The slim back mudguard of a pedal cycle is not spacious enough to show up well at a distance; but a huge white diamond on the tailboard of a lorry, or a smaller diamond on the back of a cyclist's or pedestrian's coat would unquestionably save quite a lot of lives per annum. Personally, I am whitening my waders; I refuse to disfigure a brand-new motor cycle with amateur brushing out of a tin.

12 October 1939

1934—and the clouds begin to lift

Perhaps New Hudson had tried to do too much at once, but there is a subtle irony in the fact that at just about the time the enclosed-engine New Hudson range was bowing out of the scene, what was to prove the most successful of all the enclosed models was making its entrance. That machine was the well-loved Francis-Barnett Cruiser, new for the 1933 season and totally unlike anything that factory had so far produced.

Why Francis-Barnett should have succeeded where others had come to grief is a little hard to determine, but style, and cleanliness of line, must have had a lot to do with it. The Cruiser looked exactly right for its purpose, which was a modestly powered, all-weather machine for gentlemanly touring.

In pre-war times there was no such being in the engineering world as a professional stylist, but there was a well-known adage that what looked right was right. Designer of the Cruiser was Bill King, a practical motor cyclist who served as his own test rider, and not only was he a common sight around Coventry in his long, leather riding coat but he also appeared on the cover of Francis-Barnett catalogues, the subject of a pen-and-ink sketch of a Cruiser rider in cap and coat.

Gordon Francis and Arthur Barnett (who was Gordon's father-in-law) had always had a reputation for practical unorthodoxy – their pin-joint-frame two-strokes of the 1920s were made that way for ease of dismantling and reassembly, to suit far-flung export markets. But the Cruiser was the firm's most way-out model yet, being constructed almost entirely from pressed-steel sections. That, in turn, reflected the fact that they had acquired a subsidiary concern, Clarendon Pressings Ltd, with the equipment and experience to produce sheet metalwork and pressings for Coventry's car industry.

Growth of that side of the business gave Francis-Barnett the confidence to explore the use of presswork in motor cycle construction, and from the Cruiser of 1933 onward there would be a whole family of machines incorporating pressed-steel frame and front-fork members.

However, the frame of Bill King's masterpiece was not entirely of pressed steel, because the front-down member was an I-section steel forging incorporating the steering head, in much the same way that Greeves in post-war years would employ a cast-light-alloy beam for the same purpose. Remaining members were channel section, forming a duplex chassis in which sat a 249 cc Villiers twin-port two-stroke engine.

Very deeply valanced mudguards at front and rear (the rear one completely detachable after releasing four wing nuts, to give immediate access to the rear wheel) and designed-for-the-job legshields pointed the clean-riding theme. But above all there were curvaceous bonnets encasing the lower part of the engine, the primary drive and the gearbox, held together by knurled thumbscrews. The bonnets married beautifully with the lines of the smoothly rounded cast-light-alloy expansion box which sat across the front of the engine. Twin exhaust pipes from the engine discharged into the expansion box, from the base of which a single pipe led to a flat, fishtailed silencer at the right-hand rear of the machine.

Riding comfort was assured by a large pan-type

Minister of Transport Leslie Hore-Belisha (whose name is perpetuated in the 'Belisha Beacons' of pedestrian crossings) samples a 250 cc rear-sprung Coventry-Eagle Pullman, after declaring the 1934 London Motor Cycle Show officially open

Unit-construction of engine and gearbox was a speciality of the New Imperial company in the 1930s. Most were overhead-valve, but a rarity was the 499 cc side-valve Model 80, new for the 1935 season and priced at £52

petroil lubrication, or with the Villiers automatic lubrication system by which a cylindrical oil tank was pressurised from the engine crankcase by way of a pipe embodying a one-way ball valve. An adjusting screw on the oil tank top controlled delivery to the engine, and the whole system worked very well indeed (Villiers featured it for half a dozen years) just so long as the various joints and glands remained airtight.

It is a measure of the rightness of the specification that the Cruiser was to remain in the Francis-Barnett company's list right up to the outbreak of the Second World War. In that six-year period of production it was to benefit by steady improvement, gaining in the course of time a deeper and more handsome fuel tank, a four-speed foot-change gearbox and, in the coveted J45 version, a flat-top-piston Villiers engine incorporating the Schnürle loop-scavenging system.

That the Cruiser did not return to the market when peace came again was a matter of deep regret, and although pleading letters poured into the Lower Ford Street works, the problem was that Villiers were no longer building a suitable 249 cc engine. In the course of time the Cruiser name did indeed return, gracing a model with AMC power unit, and with glass-fibre skirts covering the rear wheel. But that was not the same thing at all.

Francis-Barnett were certainly not the only manufacturers to go in for enclosure and pressed-steel frame components. Their near-neighbours,

saddle, and 3·25 in-section tyres. An instrument panel on the handlebar incorporated a lockable ignition-and-lighting switch (a real novelty in 1933), ammeter, and ignition warning light. As originally announced, the Cruiser could be supplied with

Comprehensive enclosure of the working parts permitted a machine to be cleaned by passing a hosepipe over it, while at the same time the rider could dispense with the need for special riding gear. No factory carried out the theme more successfully than Francis-Barnett, whose 250 cc Cruiser was popular from its introduction in 1933 to the outbreak of the Second World War

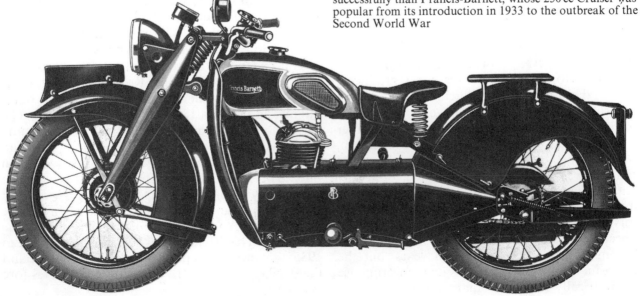

Coventry Eagle, had been marketing utility two-strokes, in pressed frames made for them by the Rubery Owen plant, since 1927. They added a model which shoe-horned a 250 cc ohv JAP engine into the same rather cramped frame. In the meantime Arthur Woodman, who had been responsible for design of the enclosed New Hudsons, had joined the Coventry Eagle company. The outcome was a very superior pressed-steel machine of rather different concept, labelled the Coventry Eagle Pullman two-seater. The engine was again the 249 cc Villiers (although, for 1935, there was the choice of an alternative power unit, a 250 cc ohv Blackburne made exclusively for Coventry Eagle), but here it was housed in a chassis rather than a frame, the side members of which extended rearward well beyond the rear wheel. Lighter pressed-steel struts supported the fuel tank and saddle.

In the first Pullman model, the rear wheel was carried on long laminated springs mounted externally to the chassis sides, but this arrangement was later modified to bring the springs within the chassis assembly. Completely covered in at each side, the rear mudguard sat on the chassis, from which it was readily detachable, and at its apex carried a shapely and comfortable-looking pillion seat which justified the machine's 'two-seater' appellation.

Production by Villiers of a new water-cooled 249 cc engine led both Excelsior and (surprise!) Vincent-HRD to introduce semi-enclosed machines powered by this unit. Known as the Viking, the Excelsior version carried enclosure to even greater lengths than either Francis-Barnett or Coventry Eagle, for the whole of the sides from footrest height to the underside of the fuel tank were hidden behind louvred panels, which also embodied inbuilt leg-shields.

Vincent-HRD had earlier experimented with a water-cooled single employing a 600 cc side-valve JAP engine but, perhaps fortunately, that remained in prototype form only and was never produced. However, the water-cooled Villiers version – which gave customers the 'plus' of cantilever rear springing – did reach the market as the Model W. One other user of the water-cooled Villiers deserves mention, because in truth the engine was initially their own design; this was SOS – a trade-mark which originally indicated Super Onslow Special, but was later adapted to So Obviously Superior. Based at a village factory just outside Worcester, Len Vale-Onslow had been building water-cooled two-strokes in both 172 cc and 249 cc sizes for several years, but the major point about the 'Soss' was its pioneering use of an electrically-welded tubular frame.

By the start of 1934, Britain's unemployment figures had dropped by a substantial 600,000, and with a little more money around the demand for motor cycles was increasing; one snag was that because of the limited output of the previous three years, good second-hand machines were as rare as hen's teeth. On the legislative side there was good news and bad news. The good news was a further reduction in motor cycle road tax, by which one-fifties would now pay 12s (60p) a year, two-fifties £1 2s 6d (£1·12½p), and over-two-fifties an annual rate of £2 5s (£2·25p).

Continuing the good news theme, the British Chancellor of the Exchequer had an unexpected Easter present for all road-users, when a Budget surplus permitted him to drop fuel tax by a penny a gallon.

On the export side our factories had despatched a hefty £1,121,000-worth of machines and parts in the twelve months up to 31 December, 1933, and while it was no surprise to find that Australia was the best export customer at £120,000-worth nor, for that matter, that South Africa was in second spot, the third-best customer was an eye-opener because it was Germany, no less! However, the exports to Germany had not all been complete machines, because quite a number of the German factories were fitting JAP or Sturmey-Archer engines, Druid forks, and other British-made accessories.

In any case, a new and harsher regime had taken over in Germany, and one of the first measures was the imposition of very heavy import duties on foreign-made goods. A significant result was that at the 1934 Berlin Show not a single foreign-built bike was to be seen. Star of the show was a new 500 cc parallel-twin two-stroke with electric starting from DKW, while Zundapp had followed DKW in adopting the Schnürle loop-scavenge principle in conjunction with flat-topped pistons.

The bad news (or at any rate, rather less good news) was the passing of the Road Traffic Act, 1934. This would not come into force immediately, but it did mean that from 18 March, 1935, there would be a speed limit of 30 mph in built-up areas. Exceeding the speed limit would, upon conviction, mean an endorsement of the driving licence – as would an offence of careless driving. Driving licences would be issued only to those who had passed a driving test successfully (but those already holding a licence issued before April, 1934, would be exempt from the necessity). The driving test would come into force in 1935, together with a provisional driving licence and the displaying of red 'L' (for 'Learner') plates fore and aft.

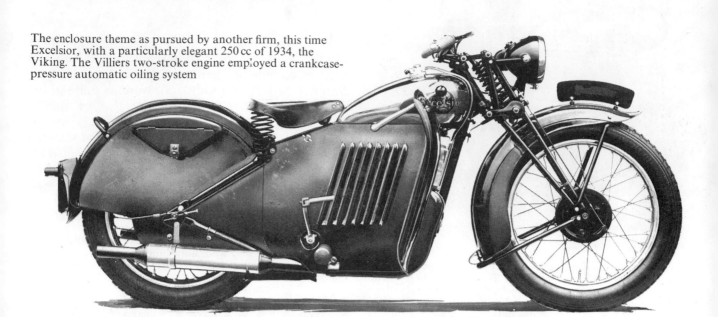

The enclosure theme as pursued by another firm, this time Excelsior, with a particularly elegant 250 cc of 1934, the Viking. The Villiers two-stroke engine employed a crankcase-pressure automatic oiling system

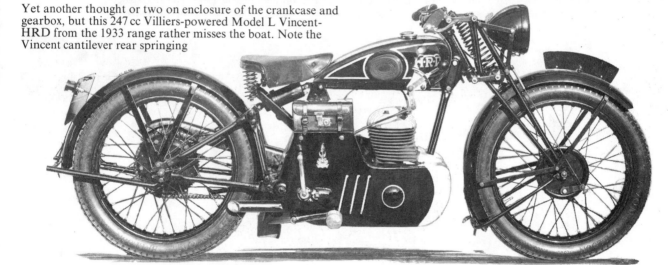

Yet another thought or two on enclosure of the crankcase and gearbox, but this 247 cc Villiers-powered Model L Vincent-HRD from the 1933 range rather misses the boat. Note the Vincent cantilever rear springing

One of the classier two-strokes of its day was the SOS, usually powered by a water-cooled Villiers engine of 150, 172, or (as here in a 1933 example) 249 cc. Unique for its time was the all-welded duplex frame of Accles and Pollock aircraft tubing. SOS were pioneers, too, of the high-level exhaust system

A colossal entry of 3,500 riders (among them Stanley Woods) took part in the Winter Rose Rally held in conjunction with the Italian Motor Cycle Show in Milan, and they, too, were to share in the good news bonanza. From the lips of Benito Mussolini in person they heard that Italy was to follow Germany's example by freeing motor cycles of all capacities from road tax; more than that, motor cycle driving licences would be abolished entirely.

Above: many a designer, over the years, has dreamt of the 'car on two wheels' but only Whitwood, from 1933 to 1935, tried to put one in production. Built by OEC, of Portsmouth, the Whitwood Monocar featured tandem bucket seats, OEC Duplex steering, and retractable outrigger wheels. A choice of engines from 250 to 996 cc was listed, but no more than half a dozen examples were ever sold

Below: pre-war grass-track passengers led an acrobatic life, as evidenced by the antics of Frank Lillie, crewman on B. Ducker's 596 cc Norton outfit. In this particular Brands Hatch race, which they won, Lillie injured his knee, collapsed, and had to be held in place by the driver as they crossed the finish line!

Bottom: midfield trio in a 350 cc event at Brands Hatch Grass Speedway in 1936. No. 131 is S. R. Williams (AJS), coming through on the inside is Don Overall (Velocette), and Epsom dealer Arthur Wheeler brings up the rear

General view of the 1934 Olympia Show with, in the immediate foreground, two of the then-new Raleigh Safety Seven three-wheelers (the ancestor of the present-day Reliant Robin). The large letter 'M' identifies the Matchless stand

With the recovery in trade, designers began to shake free of the fetters of austerity and to indulge in a few wilder flights of fancy. And there was nothing more fanciful than the Whitwood Monocar, product of that home of misplaced ingenuity, OEC. Designed by Fred Wood of OEC, the Whitwood was a real car-on-two-wheels complete with plywood bodywork, steering wheel, windscreen, and tandem seating. The engine lived under the rear seat and, to customer's choice, could be anything from a 250 cc Villiers to a 750 cc vee-twin JAP. Outrigger wheels kept the thing upright while stationary, but these swung upwards when the vehicle was under way.

It is doubtful if any more than half a dozen Whitwoods were sold in all, even though the manufacturers tried for two years to find a market. Science fiction writers, giving us a vision of the city of the future, sometimes show the streets filled with

totally enclosed two-wheeled city cars. It's a nice idea, but . . .

Almost equally exotic was William Cull's creation for the Scott company, an in-line water-cooled three which began life as a 750 cc, but developed into a massive-looking 1,000 cc with pannier fuel tanks slung astride the rear wheel. Again, only a few were made, although the engine design was revived in the early 1960s for motor boat use.

An unhappy TT experience with bought-out engines led Phil Vincent to go in for a unit of his own manufacture, and the new 500 cc high-camshaft single, for which Phil Irving was largely responsible, made its debut at the Olympia Show in a choice of standard, sports, or TT trim.

That show was to offer the visitor quite an array of inspiring work, by one maker after another. In particular there was Britain's first transverse flat-twin with integral gearbox and shaft final drive, the 494 cc Douglas Endeavour. William Douglas had just regained control of the Bristol works after yet another 'financial reconstruction', and he needed something spectacular to give the name a boost. In

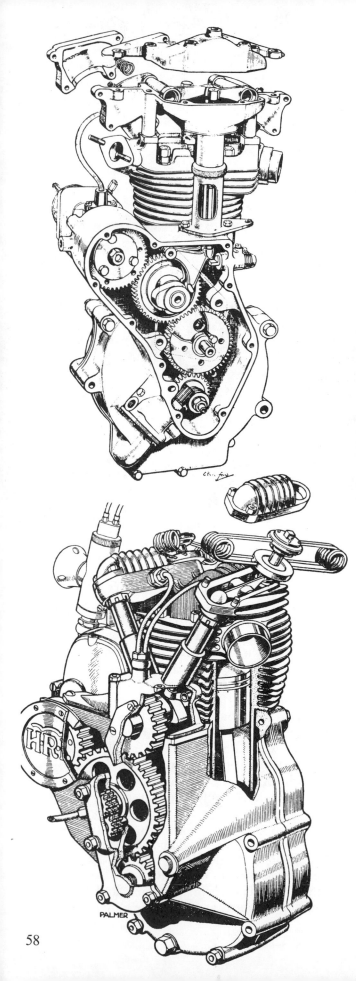

Top, left: the 248 cc Model MOV of 1934 was the first of the Velocette high-camshaft ohv models. To reduce mechanical noise, the straight-cut timing gears were soon to be replaced by helical-teeth gears

Above: exhibited in partly-cutaway form on the 1934 Norton stand at the Olympia Show was the latest 490 cc ohv International engine. Hairpin valve springs were a new-season feature

Left: an unhappy experience with bought-out engines in the 1934 TT races led Vincent-HRD to design and manufacture their own engines. This is the 1935 498 cc Comet single, with enclosed rocker arms but exposed hairpin valve springs

Opposite, top, left: undoubted sensation of the 1933 Olympia Show was the prototype 500 cc BSA with fluid-flywheel transmission and Wilson pre-selector gearbox. A selling price was announced, but the machine failed to go into production

Opposite, top, right: known as the 'Two-of-Everything', the 1934 JAP 996 cc vee-twin employed a separate downdraught carburettor, and BTH magneto, for each cylinder. It was used by Brough Superior and, to special order, Zenith

Opposite, lower: the 1934 chain-driven-ohc 250 cc Levis, designed by Ray Mason. The camshaft drive chain is automatically tensioned and lubricated

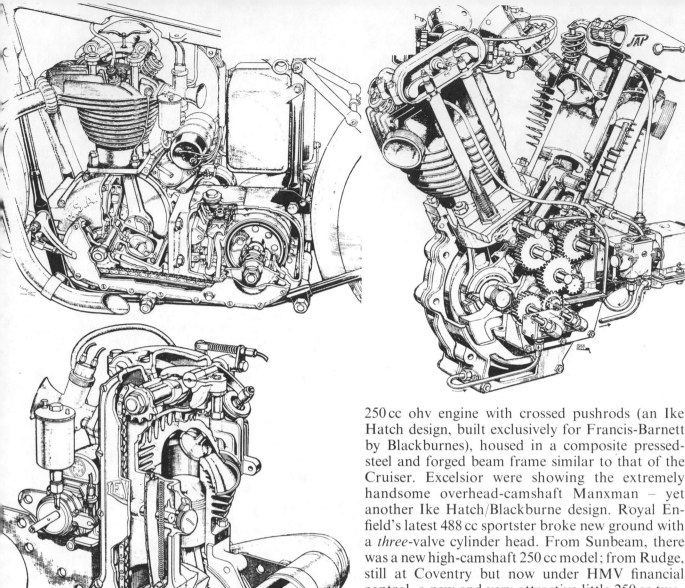

250 cc ohv engine with crossed pushrods (an Ike Hatch design, built exclusively for Francis-Barnett by Blackburnes), housed in a composite pressed-steel and forged beam frame similar to that of the Cruiser. Excelsior were showing the extremely handsome overhead-camshaft Manxman – yet another Ike Hatch/Blackburne design. Royal Enfield's latest 488 cc sportster broke new ground with a *three*-valve cylinder head. From Sunbeam, there was a new high-camshaft 250 cc model; from Rudge, still at Coventry but now under HMV financial control, a new and very attractive little 250 cc two-valver was a breakaway from the firm's four-valve tradition. Villiers offered a flat-top 250 cc engine with Schnürle loop-scavenging, which gave 12 bhp at 5,000 rpm (this may not sound much today, but for Villiers was a remarkable advance).

All in all, 1934 had been a pretty memorable year. Memorable enough, anyway, for *The Motor Cycle* to bring out, that December, a British Supremacy number in which it was pointed out that in the German, Italian, Belgian, French, Spanish, Swedish and Swiss Grands Prix plus, of course, the Isle of Man TT races, British machines had been entered in 23 classes – and had scored no fewer than 18 wins, plus countless second and third places. British industry, too, was top of the motor cycle world and, in the twelve-month period had exported three times the number of machines as those exported by Germany, France and the USA put together.

All the same, Germany was beginning to get just a bit too big for her riding boots. At Gyon, in

something under three weeks, Eddie Withers and Jack Clapham evolved the Endeavour although, because of the time factor, they had to cut a number of corners. The engine, for instance, was just the standard Blue Chief unit turned at right-angles, while the rear wheel crownwheel and bevel shaft were Morris Family Eight car components – and not genuine Morris items at that, but pattern spares.

A further Olympia Show surprise came from Francis-Barnett, with their first four-stroke for many years. This was the Stag, which featured a

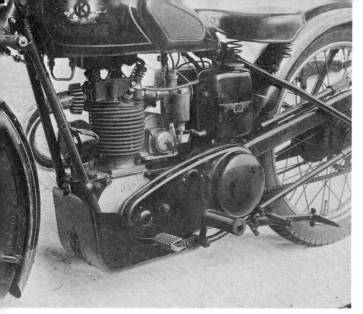

Hungary, Ernst Henne had wheeled out a Zoller-blown 750 cc BMW, to break his own existing motor cycle world speed record by clocking 152·901 mph over the flying kilometre.

Besides, Germany had won the International Six Days Trial Trophy for the second time in succession, which meant that she was entitled to organise the event in her own land again for 1935. All that flag-wagging and speech-making, and swastika signs everywhere – it was getting rather disturbing . . .

Below: William Cull's masterpiece, the three-cylinder Scott in its 1937 750 cc guise. The production version employed a 1,000 cc engine, pannier fuel tanks astride the rear wheel, and a dummy 'tank' shielding the upper part of the engine. The front fork is a Brampton-Monarch

Bottom: the story has it that the vee-twin Vincent-HRD Rapide was the outcome of a happy accident, when two tracings of the single-cylinder Comet engine were placed on a desk in such a way that they indicated a narrow twin. The machine pictured, DUR99, was the first Vincent twin to be built in running order (as opposed to a mock-up for photographic reasons), in 1938

Above: cheap, but good value for money, were the OK Supreme models produced by the Humphries family. The picture shows the 1935 Model 70, with 250 cc JAP ohv engine and the fashionable upswept exhaust system. The spring-up prop stand was a novelty

Shadows over the ISDT

Super-efficiently organised by the DDAC (Der Deutsche Automobil Club) and the NSKK (National Socialistiche Kraftfahr Korps) in the Black Forest and Bavarian Alps, the 1935 International Six Days Trial had resulted in a thoroughly convincing win for the host nation. For the third year, Germany had won the prestigious International Trophy, and to that had added the secondary team award, the International Vase.

Summing up the event in the following week's issue of *The Motor Cycle*, 'Ambleside' (the pen name used by Blick Hodgson) wrote: 'Over here we are apt to think of a trial as a happy-go-lucky affair with stretches of hard riding interspersed with a few easy checks. And in my humble opinion this was largely the cause of the somewhat disappointing show put up by the British competitors as a whole ... the close-check system was evolved with the particular idea of enabling the reliable machine to win a gold, and weeding out any that called for constant tinkering. It is this point which has been missed by a number of critics of this year's International.'

Certainly there was nothing happy-go-lucky about the way countries such as Germany or Czechoslovakia tackled the ISDT in the second part of the 1930s. The event was no longer a form of sport, but a propaganda vehicle for the regime, and whereas a British edition of the trial would be organised by a group of enthusiastic amateurs, fighting the prejudices of local and national authorities and with a total lack of either appreciation or co-operation from those in power, a German equivalent was a very different matter. The whole weight of the Nazi government would be thrown into the staging of a trial planned and regimented down to the last detail. At every corner or crossing along the route there would be storm troopers wearing swastika armbands. In many instances whole stretches of main road would be closed to everyday traffic. A well-drilled staff operated the press office, issuing copious progress bulletins in several languages to journalists covering the event. A special Post Office was brought into operation.

But perhaps it should be explained that the International Six Days Trial is not a trial in the

At that time 'Prime Minister' of Germany, Hermann Goering is seen in 1935 at a ball held to raise funds for the Berlin State Theatre. First prize in the raffle was the 400 cc BMW single seen in the foreground; Goering drew the winning ticket, but it is not known if he ever rode the bike!

observed-section sense, but is more akin to an enduro, a long-distance scramble, or the car people's Monte Carlo Rally. Time is the criterion, with manner of performance mattering not one jot. A long day's ride – possibly 200 to 300 miles of third class roads and mountain trails – would be broken up by time controls at which the card carried by each rider would be inserted into a punch clock. Penalty for lateness at a control (after a three-minute allowance) amounted to one mark per minute. A rider finishing the whole six days without time penalties would earn a gold medal, with lesser

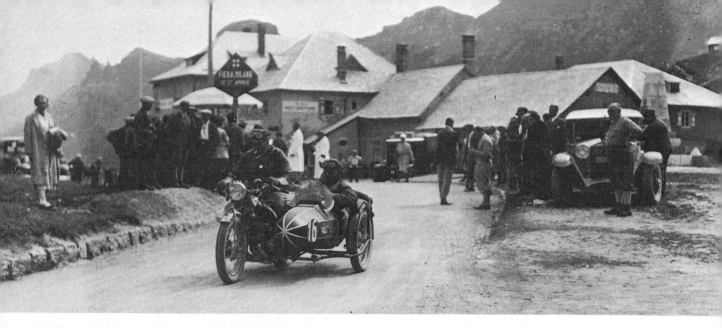

awards of silver or bronze medals for those finishing within specific totals of marks lost.

The major contest was for the International Trophy, and at this particular period it was open only to officially-entered teams of three men – two on solos, one driving a sidecar outfit – mounted on machines manufactured in the country of which they were the representatives. The lesser International

Top: 1931 ISDT. Britain's ISDT hopes plummetted on the first day when Harry Perrey (497 Ariel s/c) had to drop out with a sheared camwheel key during the afternoon section. Here he leaves the lunchtime control at the top of the Pordoi Pass

Above: British Trophy team man George Rowley (498 AJS) checks his time card before having it stamped at a second-day control point in the 1931 ISDT, held in Italy

1931 ISDT. The Italian riders relied on lightweights, such as the 175cc ohc MAS, here piloted on the Pordoi Pass by Vase A rider Egidio Picozzi

Vase contest also required three-man teams, but here they could be mounted on machines of any nationality, a stipulation which allowed countries like Ireland, with no home-based motor cycle industry, to take part.

Derived from the ACU Six Days Trial, the very first International Six Days Trial was held in the Lake District of Northern England in 1913. The series was resumed after the First World War, with Britain usually the winner of the International Trophy, but it must be said that the events were mainly of an easy-going nature.

The first ISDT of the modern series took place in France in 1930 and was based at Grenoble. Amazingly, it was very much a one-man show, with George Printam as organiser on behalf of the French governing body. M. Printam seemed to pop up here, there and everywhere, riding a solo Terrot and personally checking the efficiency of the route marking. Described by some riders as the Alpine Grand Prix, the trial was certainly a hairy affair, with high-speed schedules and steep and narrow passes.

Inevitably there were numerous crashes, and in one of these F. P. Dickson, of the Brough Superior works team, smashed his ankle against a roadside rock. Team-mates Eddy Meyer and George Brough retired themselves from the event in order to fetch help but, unfortunately, George met a large American car head-on and suffered a broken leg. Dickson later died as the result of neglected treatment to his injury. Riding a Royal Enfield, Den Welch lost an argument with a Ford car during the second day's run, and patching up the machine took so long that

he was faced with a nightmare ride, lightless, across the Goule Noire.

After two days, Italy and Britain were the only Trophy teams still unpenalised, but the third day's run saw the end of Britain's hopes when the rear wheel of Harry Perrey's Ariel sidecar outfit collapsed completely. So Italy took the Trophy (and France the Vase) and in spite of the overall toughness of the event the organisers gathered bouquets of praise for their efforts – and not a single protest.

So the pattern had been set. As 1930 winners, Italy were given the honour of staging the 1931 trial, and again it was a high-speed chase in the mountains, this time based on Merano. Time stages were really tight, and it was this fact which sent the British team out of the running on the first day. Again the unlucky man was Harry Perrey, who had to make a lightning stop to avoid hitting a car. So far, so good; but another outfit had been sitting on Harry's tail and he *didn't* stop. Crunch! The Ariel's rear mudguard was flattened against the tyre, and several minutes were lost before it could be heaved clear enough for the wheel to revolve.

Harry hared off, intent on making up time, but the hectic pace proved too much for the transmission, and the engine shaft driving key sheared before he reached the next checkpoint. Now the main team battle was between Italy and Germany, but a day or two later it seemed that Germany's chance was lost. Riding a Zündapp outfit, J. von Krohn slammed into a local car at a corner and, immediately, a crowd of excited spectators leaped forward to straighten out the machine and get von Krohn going again. That, however, counted as 'outside assistance', and at the end of the day von Krohn found himself marked as 'excluded'.

The rider protested that the 'outside assistance'

had been neither asked for nor wanted, the exclusion was remitted, and the German team was again complete; however, the incident had caused von Krohn to lose several minutes, and this was to prove vital in deciding the destination of the International Trophy. Although he was riding as an individual entry rather than a team man, Geoff Shepherd, too, had had a hair-raising experience when his Norton outfit hit a mountain road wall. Geoff was knocked out for several minutes, and the machine was decidedly second-hand, but after a while he remounted and rode the 140 miles back to base – and that included descending the 46 hairpin turns of the Stelvio Pass – in a groggy condition, and with the horn and both brakes out of action.

The Trophy went to Italy again, with Holland taking the Vase, and in consequence Merano was again the venue for the 1932 meeting. For once, luck went Britain's way (although not for Fred Neill, of the Matchless works team, who dashed into a time control with the bike on fire, only to find that no fire extinguisher was available; the disconsolate Fred had to watch the machine burn itself out).

Victory for the British Vase team was clear cut, but the Trophy squad finished the trial level-pegging with Italy, with both teams retaining clean sheets. Everything depended on the speed test, the traditional sixth-day element in which riders had to maintain (or if possible improve upon) their allotted speed schedules. After the individual entries had run their course the track was cleared, and the two Trophy teams – Bert Perrigo (BSA), George Rowley (AJS) and Peter Bradley (Sunbeam sidecar) for Britain, and Rosalino Grana, Miro Maffeis and Luigi Gilera (all on side-valve Gileras, with Luigi as the sidecar exponent) – took station on the line.

An intermittent misfire caused Perrigo to drop behind schedule, but the other two Britons had enough in hand to more than make up the deficit, and so Britain was back on top of the heap, with both Trophy and Vase in the bag.

It was therefore the turn of the ACU to organise the 1933 event, and the selected headquarters town was Llandrindod Wells, in mid-Wales, a spa town with the advantages of ample hotel accommodation and reasonable closeness to mountain going. With considerably less rough going available than had been evident in the Italian and French events, the ACU did their best but, inevitably, riders had an easier time of it except at Dinas Rock, a narrow hill which became choked with struggling competitors and thereby led to the abandonment of one timed section. During the third day's run, news spread rapidly that world speed record holder Ernst Henne,

riding for Germany's International Trophy team, had dropped a mark through stopping to repair a puncture – but any jubilation in the British camp was short-lived because during a downpour that same afternoon George Rowley had missed a vital piece of route marking, had gone off course, and was two marks down.

Those two marks could not be made up, and for the first time, the name of 'Deutschland' was inscribed on the Trophy. To Germany, too, went the privilege of organising the 1934 ISDT, the Garmisch-Partenkirchen area being selected to host the event.

At this point, though, it is necessary to look outside the realm of motor cycle sport, at the political situation in Germany. After an unsuccessful attempt to take over power in 1923, Adolf Hitler and his Nazi party seized their chance ten years later. In 1933, Hitler became Chancellor of Germany, and from that point on things moved with alarming rapidity. Loyal party members were rewarded with positions of high office, while those who opposed Hitler's policies were eliminated.

Just how efficient was the process of elimination was made very evident to motor cyclists when the front row of the grandstand at the 1934 German Grand Prix, reserved for an impressive list of notables, was seen to be almost empty. On the previous evening, more than half of these who were to have attended in the place of honour had been 'purged' – bloodily and very, very permanently.

The Nazis now looked at the sport of motor cycling, a sport which by its very nature attracted young men of an adventurous spirit. Here, then, was a group ripe for moulding into the image of the master race. Among Hitler's closest associates was an ex-Major named Huhnlein, who had been at his side in the abortive 'putsch' of 1923. Currently the representative of a tyre factory, Huhnlein had a genuine love of motor sport, and now Hitler gave him the title of Sportführer and the job of organising motoring and motor cycling along Nazi lines.

Officially, Germany had been represented in international councils by the DDAC, a democratic body on the same lines as Britain's ACU, but Huhnlein now created the NSKK, a drilled and disciplined motorised section of the Brownshirts. Overall control of motor and motor cycling sport was to be in the hands of the ONS (Oberste Nationale Sporthörde), a politically controlled body which edged the DDAC more and more to one side until it had virtually eliminated it. From that point on, competitive motor cycling had little connection with sport and became frankly military by nature.

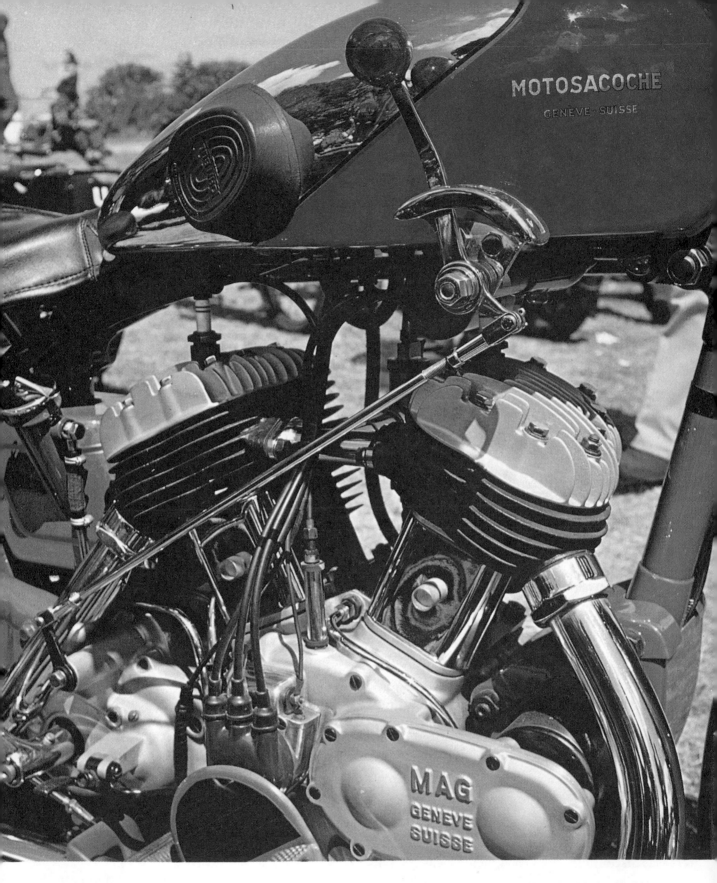

Pride of Switzerland was the Motosacoche, which hailed from Geneva (the same factory supplied proprietary engines, under the MAG trademark, to many other motor cycle builders).

This 850 cc vee-twin side-valve of 1932, with detachable cylinder heads, is one of many immaculate examples in the Eric Bezon collection

Corresponding to Germany's Nazis were the Fascisti of Italy, faithful followers of motor-cycle-fanatic Benito Mussolini. In this shot a parade of Fascist Youth gymnasts is inspected by an official on a Moto Guzzi horizontal single, in 1934

There were two reasons for this. First there was the Nazi creed that Germany had to be seen to excel in every possible field. 'Success ... success ... success ...' squawked Goebbels, Hitler's propaganda chief; and it was Huhnlein's responsibility that, so far as motor cycling was concerned, Germany won everything that was going.

The second reason was rather more sinister. A time would come, now only a few short years ahead, when the country would have need of a vast reserve of motor cyclists trained in cross-country going, to spearhead the German Army's lightning sweeps into enemy territory.

Korpsführer Huhnlein was given a substantial budget, and with this a number of two- and three-day trials on ISDT lines were organised. Riders showing particular promise were picked out for all-the-year-round training camps in the mountains, where they were brainwashed into the code that they had to win every time, and that a beaten team meant disgrace for the Fatherland.

To encourage motor cycling in general, *all* road tax on two-wheelers and sidecar outfits was waived. Unnecessary rivalry between German manufacturers was discouraged, and each factory was given its own brief concerning the lines along which development should travel. Teams representing the German Army were entered for whatever trials were on offer, with the full backing of mobile workshops, and corps of helpers at every control. Major national events were bedecked with Nazi flags and banners, brass bands playing martial tunes, and addresses by party leaders.

The Nazification of the sport was certainly in evidence at Garmisch-Partenkirchen in 1934, although it had yet to reach its full and most ominous flowering. Germany's International Trophy team, all on BMW twins, comprised the old firm of Henne, Josef Stelzer and Ludwig Kraus while, once again, the Italians relied on their Gilera-mounted trio. Britain, too, had an unchanged trio – and, once more, it was on Bert Perrigo that the fates frowned. High on a mountain track, his BSA picked up a climber's boot nail through one tyre, and even though the tyres of all the British teamsters had been treated beforehand with liquid rubber sealing compound, this failed to act. Bert ripped out the punctured tube and inserted a spare, but the liquid sealant had spread around the inside of the cover, acting as a lubricant. As the BSA set off again, so the tyre spun round on the rim, tearing the valve from the tube. Frantically, Bert fitted a second spare. This time it held, but a precious minute was lost at the next time control. Britain's Vase 'A' team (there was a 'B' team, too, from the Scottish ACU) was also suffering, losing Jack Williams when the gearbox of his Norton packed in, and sidecar man Harold Flook when he struck a roadside milestone and wiped off the sidecar wheel and axle.

That year, the highspot of the trial had been the Somerberg, a hill where over half the entry had had to be pushed up. But Germany had won again and,

so far as the Nazis were concerned, that was the entire object of the exercise.

If Nazificiation had been a feature of the 1934 event, it was nothing to what 1935 produced. Now the Nazi banners and swastika armbands were everywhere, storm troopers 'Heil Hitlered' and exchanged raised-arm salutes on every possible occasion, and woe betide any poor unfortunate who got in the way.

To give just one example, British Vase 'A' team man Jack Williams rounded a corner of a narrow lane to find himself heading for an oncoming sidecar outfit – in fact the breakdown outfit of a local garage, ridden by a rather dim youth. All Jack could do was fling himself into the nearest hedge and let the Norton have the accident on its own; which it did, quite thoroughly. Police were soon on the spot – and it was the sidecar driver who was hauled off to jail unceremoniously!

Determined to win, Germany had equipped her Trophy team with brand-new 500 cc overhead-camshaft BMWs fitted with Zoller superchargers and telescopic front forks. Again, the riders were Kraus, Stelzer and Henne, and now there was a Vase team, too, comprising Walfried Winkler, Arthur Geiss, and Ewald Kluge – in fact, the DKW works road-racing team – all riding 250 cc DKWs.

Incidents there were, in plenty. Riding for the

eam, Karl Gall shot off the road into a ditch, partly stunning himself; in a confused state he hauled his BMW back to the roadway, and restarted but in the wrong direction of the course, colliding with British privateer John Sinclair (Calthorpe) and so causing a double retirement. Kraus, the sidecar man of the Trophy squad, upended his BMW outfit and knocked out passenger P. Müller but, undismayed, dumped the spark-out crewman in the chair and rode on to the finish of the day's run, six miles away.

The next day, after treatment, Müller was back in the chair and away went the pair. Again Kraus overturned, and this time Müller collected a broken rib. But 'win at all costs' was the motto, and that applied also to Walfried Winkler, of Germany's DKW-riding Vase team, who came off and broke a toe. A police motor cyclist stopped to render assistance and, to cover the swollen toe, offered Winkler his own (rather larger) riding boot. Nor was that the end of the tale, because rumour had it that the cop, now with one stockinged foot, later pushed over another policeman and grabbed *his* boot!

Thousands of marks had been spent on the final speed test circuit, where there were straw bales and sandbags at every few yards. Of the initial 254 entries, 138 had survived to the last day, among them British private entry Billy Tiffen, down to collect his ninth consecutive gold medal. Sid Moran (Matchless) also appeared to have the gold medal in his pocket but when the flag fell to start his section of the speed test, the Matchless just sulked. At the worst

ISDT 1935. Chief of the Nazi Civil Corps at Oberstdorf, The Duke of Saxe-Coburg-Gotha inspects the Brownshirts who were to act as marshals for the trial, prior to delivering a speech of welcome to foreign riders

BSA's big side-valve twin, the 986 cc Model G32-10, was essentially a sidecar haulier, but is seen here in solo form. New for 1932 were detachable cylinder heads with heart-shaped combustion chambers, which were claimed to give a 25 per cent boost in power output. New, also, was the tank-top instrument panel and the 'semi-American' handlebars

Charged with the job of producing something new and exciting for the Douglas stand at the 1934 Olympia Show – but in a tearing hurry and on a low budget – experimental department engineers Eddie Withers and Jack Chapman evolved the legendary 494 cc Douglas Endeavour transverse twin. The engine was simply the Blue Chief unit turned through 90 degrees and the crownwheel and pinion of the shaft drive assembly were Morris 8 pattern spares (they could not afford the genuine items). Reputedly, only 100 or so Endeavours were ever sold; a survivor is the one above, owned by Bob Thomas, of Milntown, Isle of Man

Top: the more expensive brother of the Red Panther, the 248 cc Model 70 (see page 35). The registration number indicates 1934, first year the Model 70 was listed

Bottom: the Brough Superior 800 cc water-cooled in-line four, which employed a modified Austin Seven engine and transmission; the shaft drive was located between the twin rear wheels. Ten were built, between 1932 and 1934, and six are known to survive

Top: ISDT 1935. Triumph works teamster Allan Jefferies (493 Triumph Mk. V) weighs in. He was to finish the event with a clean sheet, to win a gold medal

Above: ISDT 1935. Britain's gallant pair of lady riders. Edyth Foley (*left*) rode a 497 cc Zundapp. Unlucky Marjorie Cottle (*left*) on a 348 cc BSA had to retire when her machine caught fire and was burnt out

possible moment, the ignition had failed totally.

For all Germany's effort, it looked as though the Trophy would go to Czechoslovakia, who were three points ahead as the teams came to the line. Moreover, Josef Stelzer had clonked the cylinder head of his BMW against a rock, and though he had stemmed the torrent of oil from the broken rocker box cover with tyre patches, the repair looked decidedly dodgy.

All the Czechs, on overhead-valve Jawas, had to do was keep going steadily. But it was not to be; Vitvar's 350 cc Jawa broke a valve, the head went through the piston, and that was that. It was Deutschland Über Alles, yet again.

But a country can get over-confident, and the 1936 event saw Germany well and truly beaten on her own ground, and Britain came into her own by

snatching both the Trophy *and* the Vase. Indeed, all three British teams – Trophy men George Rowley, Vic Brittain and Stuart Waycott, Vase 'A' teamsters Jack Williams, Allan Jefferies and Len Heath, and the all-Scottish Vase 'B' team of Bob McGregor, J. C. Edward and J. A. McLeslie – finished with clean sheets, with the Scots putting up the better Speed Test showing and thereby winning the International Vase.

For 1937, therefore, the ISDT was based at Llandrindod Wells again, and for some unknown reason the ACU staged the event in July – the height of the touring season in mid-Wales – instead of the more usual September. By comparison with the efficiency of the Continentals, the British organisation was pathetic, although it must be said that the ACU hands were tied to a large degree by local police insistence that speed schedules be kept low. Yet if there was a marked lack of tough, unmetalled tracks, there were hazards in abundance in the form of dawdling holiday-makers, sheep, and motor-cycle-hating dogs. The speed test was held at Donington Park, and the main battle was, once more, between Britain (Rowley, Brittain, and Waycott) and Germany (Kraus, Stelzer, and road-race star Georg Meier). The scrap just could not have been closer, and although the Trophy went to Britain, it was by the extremely narrow margin of 10 seconds.

Although the motor cycling press urged the ACU not to take up its option of staging the 1938 event in Britain, the pleas fell on deaf ears and so, once again, Llandrindod Wells was invaded by hundreds of motor cycles. All the same, any competitor who expected to see a repeat of the easy 1937 event was very soon disillusioned. Rain poured down. It deluged. Roads were flooded, shallow fords became raging torrents. Two hills on the opening day's run became choked with exhausted riders.

Switching away from the customary BMW flat twins, Germany had taken the bold step of mounting their Trophy men on 175 cc two-stroke DKWs and relegating the erstwhile Trophyists to the Vase competition. But two of the DKW riders went out on the second day, as did one of the Czechoslovakian Trophy teamsters. Then, out along the Tregaron-Abergwesyn Pass, the sidecar wheel stub axle of Ludwig Kraus's 600 cc BMW broke away. That year, Korpsführer General Huhnlein had presented a special trophy to be competed for by military, and other organisational teams, and this had encouraged the British Army, at last, to take an interest in cross-country motor cycling. In fact, there were no fewer than 27 teams entered for the Huhnlein award,

including the Royal Tank Corps trio of Sgt J.T. Dalby, Cpl Fred Rist, and Cpl R. Gillam, all on the new M24 BSA Gold Stars, plus a trio of RAC road patrolmen, on Norton Internationals.

Inexplicably, the ACU had failed to provide alternate schedules for wet or dry conditions, and before the dreadful week was over only 28 of the original 209 starters were still motoring. For those who managed to stay on the gold standard, a special award was made; and never was award more gamely earned.

The most savage slaughter had been among the sidecar crews, with just two survivors from a field of 37. But one of those two was Stuart Waycott (495 cc Velocette) and that meant that Britain alone finished with an intact Trophy team. Compensation of a kind for Germany – and for Huhnlein, attending as Hitler's personal envoy – was the winning of the Vase, Huhnlein Trophy, and the club team prize.

Once more, the press pleaded with the ACU not to take up the option of running the 1939 trial. The risks had been little short of appalling, the speed schedules far too high for roads open to other traffic, and the whole event had been unfair on continental riders unused to hedges, high banks, and unpoliced lanes.

'There is no doubt that such international competitions help tremendously towards preserving peace', declared General Huhnlein, at the 1937 prize-presentation ceremony. But the fact that every German rider in that year's event, and the next, had been entered either by the NSKK or the German Army belied his words. In the previous German-organised events, all the military evidence had given British competitors an uncomfortable feeling that things were moving towards an inevitable conclusion. So the announcement that Germany would take over from Britain the running of the 1939 ISDT came as something of a surprise; Hitler had already marched into Austria, and into Sudetenland, and was making threatening noises in other directions. In Britain, important buildings were being given the protection of sandbag walls, there were trenches dug in public parks, and posters advised recruitment into the Territorial Army, Civil Defence, or the Auxiliary Fire Service.

Yet despite the tension, the 1939 ISDT was 'on', and the British entries – private, official Trophy and Vase, and Army – made their way across a nervous European countryside to the familiar area of Garmisch-Partenkirchen. There, the signs were even more ominous, but much to everybody's surprise the trial started. Soon, however, the situation had grown so serious that telegrams urging the return

Top: ISDT 1935. Better known as a World Motor Cycle Speed Record contender, Ernst Henne rode this supercharged 500 cc BMW as a member of the victorious German Trophy team. He is seen near Rioder, on the opening day's route

Above: ISDT 1935. Erminio Villa (499 Gilera), of the Italian Trophy team enters Grobdorf in Bavarian sunshine

immediately of all British nationals were winging towards Bavaria. To go on was tempting – Britain was by that time virtually certain of Trophy success – but the position was by now untenable, and although the German authorities offered fuel, and a safe conduct to the border, should the team decide to continue, it was felt best to cut and run for it. Already tired after a hard day's ride, the British entries clocked in at the final control, but instead of leaving their machines in the *parc fermé* they rode on to their lodgings, crammed such of their luggage as could be taken into the cars and vans of the support crews and lashed the rest to their mud-caked bikes. Then they lit out pell-mell for the frontier, before the barriers crashed down for good and all.

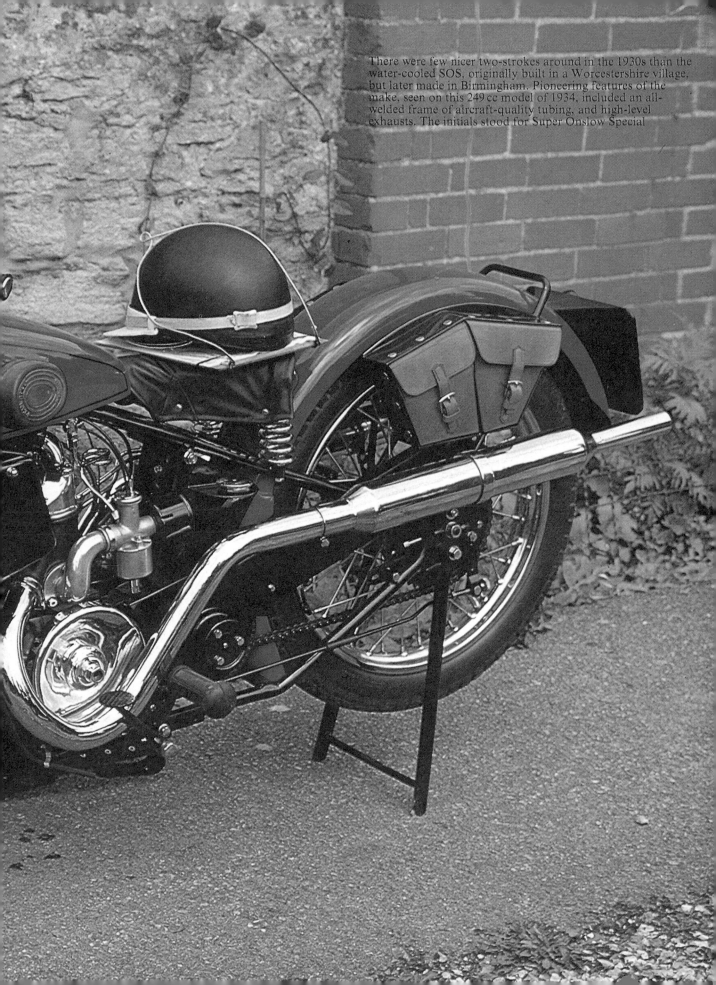

There were few nicer two-strokes around in the 1930s than the water-cooled SOS, originally built in a Worcestershire village, but later made in Birmingham. Pioneering features of the make, seen on this 249 cc model of 1934, included an all-welded frame of aircraft-quality tubing, and high-level exhausts. The initials stood for Super Onslow Special

Above: ISDT 1935. In a pre-trial survey, Len Heath (497 Ariel) looks out over the valley from the highest of the 100 hairpin bends on Oberjoch test hill. The swastika armband of the policeman, left, hints at the troubles to come in the years ahead

Right: ISDT 1935. A rarity in a continental ISDT was this supercharged Morgan three-wheeler, driven by *Motor Cycling's* Midland editor, Henry Laird. This is Immenstadt, and what seems to be a lake in the background is actually a mist-filled valley

Right, below: Georg Meier is usually thought of as a star road racer and winner of the 1939 Senior TT. Here, however, he is pictured (centre) as a member of Germany's Trophy team for the 1937 International Six Days Trial. Left is Ludwig ('Wiggerl') Kraus, and right is Josef Stelzer. All on BMW flat-twins, the team finished as runners-up to Britain

They made it, and only just in time. Next day, the radio announced that Germany had invaded Poland, and within days Britain and France were at war with Germany. Leading that advance into Poland were the motor cyclists of the Wehrmacht, trained to seize key positions and pave the way for the heavier armour; men who had learned their cross-country riding skills under the banner of sport.

'The right crowd and no crowding'

Waving the Union Jack vigorously, *The Motor Cycle* had offered a silver cup, for the first 100 miles-in-the-hour to be recorded by a British-made multi-cylinder 500 cc machine on British soil; a handsome offer, but the fly in the ointment was the 'on British soil' bit – because for anyone trying to pack a hundred miles into an hour under ACU supervision the choice was Brooklands, full stop. Nor was Brooklands, near Weybridge in Surrey, the smooth-surfaced and steeply-banked concrete bowl that one might imagine. It was, in fact, infernally bumpy.

But still, several people decided that they might as well have a crack at winning the trophy. There were Tommy Atkins, with his impressive-looking ohv Douglas twin, Ben Bickell with a blown Ariel Square Four, Tommy Spann with a works-prepared blown Triumph twin (one of the Val Page-designed 650 cc models cut down to 500 cc to meet the requirements), and Ginger Wood with yet another works machine, this time without the benefit of a supercharger. Designed by Matt Wright, this last was a vee-twin New Imperial, essentially a pair of cylinders and heads from the factory's 250 cc racing single, carried on a common crankcase.

The two forged-duralumin connecting rods of the New Imperial were mounted side-by-side on a massive crankpin (the resulting offset of the cylinders aided cooling of the rear pot), and the complete crankshaft was carried on half a dozen assorted ball and roller main bearings, including an outboard bearing beyond the engine shaft sprocket.

Unlike the other contenders, the New Imp had not been built essentially for an attempt at gaining the cup. It was a road race model, and its first outing was in the 1934 Dutch Grand Prix. The potential was there, but Ginger Wood had to retire when the windings of the twin magnetos (lying alongside the crankcase and driven by bevels) began to melt.

After a modicum of redesign, New Imperial took the bike to Brooklands but again the team ran into trouble, this time when an inlet valve stretched after six high-speed laps. Back to Birmingham went the machine, while Ginger kicked his heels and bided his time – which was a bit of bad luck for him, because while waiting for the machine to return to the track he agreed to try out a Velocette on which Noel Christmas had been working.

In his shirt sleeves he headed up Aerodrome Road, Weybridge, when suddenly a car turned across his path, and Ginger went skating up the

The atmosphere of Brooklands can almost he felt in this picture of the 1930 Brooklands Grand Prix getting under way. Every rider was allowed a personal pusher for the start. The location is The Fork, and beyond the footbridge can be seen the steep Members' Banking. The Clubhouse, left, survives in the midst of later industrial development

Coveted by sporty lads was the very neat overhead-camshaft
Excelsior Manxman, of which this is a 1936 250 cc example.
That year, 350 and 500 cc versions were added to the
catalogue, but only the two smaller-capacity machines could
be supplied in out-and-out racing trim

One of the Brooklands regulars was RAF pilot Chris Staniland, who usually rode the machines owned and prepared by J. S. Worters. Illustrated is the 250 cc Rex-Acme-Blackburne on which Chris, who always rode in white overalls, won the 1930 Brooklands 250 cc Championship at 90·27 mph. Just what the gentleman on the right is wearing under his open coat is a matter for conjecture

roadway on his back, creating so much friction that his shirt actually began to singe. He also lost a large patch of skin, but for professional riders such as Ginger every booking was valuable. He *daren't* tell the firm, or they would have signed-on somebody else. In any case, the next attempt was ten days ahead, so he had his back strapped up with bandages and hoped for the best.

On the evening of 1 August, 1934, all was ready and, to cut down on expenses, the hire of the track and the expenses of an approved timekeeper were shared between New Imperial, the Triumph squad, and Ben Bickell. Ben's Ariel was, in fact, the firm's 600 cc demonstration job, to which a 500 cc cylinder block had been fitted. The Square Four certainly had the speed to annexe the cup, but Bickell had been in endless bother, mainly with blowing cylinder head gaskets.

The New Imp, too, had its foibles, notably a tendency to oil-up on the front cylinder if revved too hard, and so Les Archer, acting as pit manager, worked out a system of human pit signals. If he stood with arms outstretched, Ginger was on schedule. If the arms dropped, he was dropping behind. If they were raised, he was getting too far ahead.

Which was all very well, but Ginger later con-

fessed that about halfway through the run he forgot which signal meant what. The New Imperial was getting ahead of itself. 'Poor old Les was flapping his arms so furiously, he almost took off,' said Ginger.

Indeed, the machine had so much power to spare that Wood could cruise round at part throttle and still hold 105 mph. There was little point in lapping at a higher speed than was strictly necessary, and in the closing stages Matt Wright and Les Archer gave the slow-down signal until Ginger was cruising at just under the 100 mph mark. That was good enough, and in due course George Reynolds, the ACU timekeeper emerged from his hut (known to all Brooklands habitues as 'Chronograph Villa') to give the New Imperial camp a thumbs-up sign.

Ginger had done it, with an average speed for the hour of 102·27 mph. And that was bad news for Tommy Spann and the Triumph brigade, because after curing some initial bothers they, too, had got their machine circulating nicely at 105 mph.

It could not be said that Ginger had won comfortably. During the run the scab of his sore back had come loose, and was sloughing up and down under his leathers. He felt, he said, like a snake that had shed its skin.

'The right crowd and no crowding' was the slogan used by Brooklands race organisers – and that could be interpreted as meaning that spectators, for motor cycle meetings, anyway, were decidedly thin on the ground. Not that the BMCRC, responsible for most motor cycle events at the Weybridge track, did very much to attract spectators. They were, for example,

One of the most successful of all Brooklands sidecar racing outfits was 'Barry's Big Blown Brough', operated by strong man Ted Baragwanath, powered by a supercharged JAP 8/50 vee-twin engine, and capable of lapping Brooklands at 108 mph

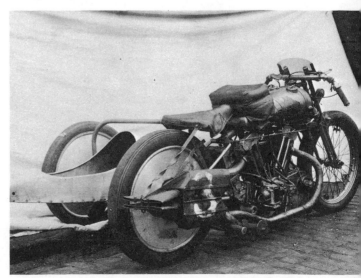

Above: Ginger Wood, pictured immediately after he had taken *The Motor Cycle* trophy by achieving 100 miles in the hour with the vee-twin New Imperial, in August, 1934

Below: the 492 cc New Imperial twin – in effect a 'double-up' of the same firm's successful 246 cc racer – was the first British multi-cylinder five-hundred to cover one hundred miles in an hour on British soil (1 August, 1934), so winning *The Motor Cycle* Cup. However, handling left a lot to be desired, and only Ginger Wood seemed able to control it. Even so, it flung him off at Brooklands when tried out in supercharged form. Charlie Dodson raced it in the 1934 Senior TT, its first outing, but a broken pushrod put him out while lying sixth

given to staging Wednesday race meetings, which may have been fine for shopkeepers in towns where Wednesday was half-day closing, but not for anybody else.

The main trouble was that Brooklands was too vast, and while there was something to enjoy in watching huge aircraft-engined cars like Count Zborowski's famous Chitty-Bang-Bang thundering round, bikes were out of scale and, as somebody once put it, looked like so-and-so flies crawling round a soup plate. Then again, Brooklands, privately built by Hugh Fortescue Locke-King on his own estate and opened in 1907, was too near the houses on St George's Hill, Weybridge. A militant residents' lobby had already ensured that the track should not be used for longer than 12 hours a day (which put paid to any 24-hour record attempts). The same residents' lobby was responsible for the huge lozenge-like silencers and fishtails – the famous Brooklands Cans – which had to be worn by every competing bike.

To liven up proceedings a little, the Mountain Circuit was introduced in 1930, taking in the Finishing Straight, and the banked section around the back of Members' Hill. For all that, a press report at the end of 1930 spoke of 'interminable waits between races.'

The track was inhabited by a body of professionals, many of them with tuning sheds actually on the spot, who had earned a little jam on their daily bread by breaking a few records now and then (but not by such a large margin that the next man would be deterred from having a go), so winning a few cheques from the makers of tyres, carburettors, and

In the eyes of many an enthusiast, the Norton International was *the* classic bike. The picture shows a beautifully restored 1936 490 cc Model 30 ohc, originally listed at £90 plus another £1 10s for the racing-type 3½-gallon fuel tank

Two-strokes were included in the Velocette range from 1913 to 1940. Seen here is the 1936 250 cc Model GTP with light-alloy cylinder head, coil ignition and foot-change gearbox.

The final batch of GTP models (250 of them, all with chain-driven magneto ignition) were built in 1940 exclusively for export markets

Top: so wide was the Brooklands track that artificial chicanes had to be introduced, just to make racing more interesting. Leader in this shot from the 1936 Brooklands Senior Grand Prix is Denis Minett (Rudge), followed by Johnny Lockett (Norton) and Jock West (Triumph)

Above: a broad grin from Eric Fernihough (175 cc Excelsior-Blackburne) as he draws level with Charles Mortimer, senior (250 cc New Imperial) in the 1934 Hutchinson 100 handicap race at Brooklands. Eric, the eventual winner, knows something that Chas has yet to discover; the New Imp's rear tyre has punctured!

so forth used on the run. These cheques were bonuses or, in the language of Brooklands, 'boni'.

But, said *The Motor Cycle* summing up the 1930 season: 'Things have been quiet at Brooklands in 1930. Throughout the year the professionals have gone about with long faces. Boni, we hear, are to be

cut down from the small amounts of 1930 to practically nothing at all, and a bonus in one form or another is the mainstay of the professional rider's existence.'

Quiet at Brooklands? Well, maybe at that time of slump, but normally there was usually something going on at the track, which was not only a race venue but the nearest thing manufacturers had to the present-day MIRA test circuit near Nuneaton. It was even possible, on certain days, to pay a few shillings and drive round in the family car, or try out the modifications you had carried out over the winter to your own motor cycle.

Possibly the oddest vehicle to be seen there in the early 1930s was the Dynasphere, a huge monowheel

within which sat the driver. Designed by a Dr Purves, it was constructed jointly by Douglas Motors and the British Aluminium Company – and rumour has it that one frosty winter's morn it skidded on a frozen pond and subsided gently into the smelliest lagoon of the infamous Brooklands sewage farm!

There was always a spate of record-attempting immediately prior to the Olympia Show, so that (hopefully) a manufacturer could have something to shout about when the show opened. Always, too, some maker or other was making a bid for the Maudes Trophy, of which more later.

Probably the most prestigious race meeting of the year was the Hutchinson 100, run in October. It was, admittedly, a complicated affair for the spectator, because it was a handicap event, and not until the closing stages did things begin to come together. 'Public address' was in its infancy, and unless the average spectator paid close attention from the start he would soon lose himself in a mass of figuring.

For example, in the Hutchinson 100 of 1931, Ben Bickell, with his 500 cc Bickell-JAP was the scratch man. But the limit man was A. H. Walker (250 Rex-Acme-Blackburne) who was given a start of no less than 18 minutes 30 sec. Solos and sidecars were mixed up together, with Fergus Anderson (499 cc Rudge sidecar) receiving a start of 16 minutes 39 sec. What it meant was that poor Ben had to sit on the sidelines while Walker did nine laps, before he was given the signal to start. In any case, the winner was Spug Muir (350 cc Velocette), who was given a start of 6 minutes 47 sec.

The following year, 1932, there was an even bigger gap between the scratch man (Bickell again) and the limit man, this time Eric Fernihough on his 175 cc Excelsior-JAP, who had been given a handsome 21 minutes 53 sec by the handicapper. Not that it did Eric much good, because he covered less than half a mile before the sorely-stressed miniature engine split the cylinder barrel from the crankcase.

It was the pleasant custom of the British Motor Cycle Racing Club (hereinafter termed Bemsee) to award a tiny gilt lapel badge in the form of a star with the figures '100' across it, to a rider lapping at over 100 mph in a meeting organised by the club – although maybe it should be said that a rider could only win his Gold Star once. Lady riders, too, were allowed to try for a Gold Star, but only on a deserted track, not in a race. This, said Bemsee, was for their

Very recognisably an ancestor of the post-war BSA B-series singles, the 1937 348 cc BSA Empire Star was yet another Val Page design. The oil pump 'blister' on the right of the crankcase was to remain a characteristic of the make for many years

own safety; but quite a few chauvinistic male riders were known to mutter that it was for *their* safety, too!

Only one 250 cc machine ever won a Gold Star, and that was an Excelsior-JAP ridden by Monty Saunders in August, 1933. The machine was completely panelled in at each side with sheet aluminium, and had been built two years earlier by J. S. Worters. However, handling in any sort of a breeze was dodgy in the extreme, and it must have been an exceptionally calm day when Saunders sped round, to set a 250 cc lap record of 102·48 mph which would never be beaten, and to cover five miles at a 102 mph average.

The Wednesday-afternoon race meetings were, to quote the contemporary press: 'Placid affairs where all the aspects of motor cycle sport were discussed in between the races, and the informal discussions were almost as interesting and important as the racing.'

But one particular Wednesday, late in June, 1937, was destined to make the semi-somnolent spectators sit up straight. The programme for that day included the name of W. L. Handley (497 cc BSA), and that was a double surprise. In the first place, Wal Handley had retired from big-time racing a season or two earlier, to devote his energies to running a motor cycle showroom in Suffolk Street, Birmingham. And in the second place, the BSA had never been considered a racing model.

The bike Wal brought to the starting line looked very standard, with its cast-iron cylinder barrel and head, and to all intents and purposes it was an Empire Star, a semi-sports job introduced a few months earlier; Val Page, formerly of the Ariel and

Triumph design departments, was responsible for the model, which was characterised by the bulge on the right of the crankcase, housing a gear-type oil pump.

The race was a three-lap Outer Circuit handicap, and quite evidently the handicapper knew a thing or two, because he put Wal on the 9 sec mark, alongside a group of fast Brooklands specialists. On the first lap he weaved his way past most of the field, by the second lap he was out in front, and on the third and final lap he stretched his lead to 100 yards, winning at an average speed of 102·27 mph, and setting a fastest lap of 107·57 mph. Magic! Handley had won a Gold Star, most decisively!

Background to the plot was that BSA intended to produce, for 1938, a new super-sports bike based on the Empire Star but with considerably more performance. Sales manager Stan Banner, and chief engineer David Munro were involved, managing director Joe Bryan gave the OK, and trials stars Len Crisp and Jack Amott prepared the machine (which, by the way, was given a 13 to 1 compression ratio). The fuel used was alcohol.

Competitions manager of BSA at the time, Bert Perrigo did the arm-twisting and persuaded Wal Handley to bring his riding leathers out of mothballs for the occasion, and so the deed was done.

After the race, Val Page got to work on his drawing board, and what emerged was an all-alloy version of the Empire Star, with cast-in pushrod tunnels. In catalogue parlance it was the Model M24. But Wal Handley's feat had given it a name that was to earn, in the years ahead, near-immortality. That name was the BSA Gold Star.

A rider who lapped Brooklands at over 100 mph in a BMCRC-promoted meeting was awarded a small Gold Star lapel badge. Wal Handley won his star in 1937 on a specially works-tuned BSA Empire Star. From that machine was evolved a new light-alloy-engine 500 cc sports model, introduced in the 1938 BSA programme as (what else!) the Gold Star

Catering for the clubman

Nobody could claim that the British would-be road racer of pre-war days was spoilt for choice in the matter of available circuits at which to brush up his skill. There was Brooklands, of course, and there was the Isle of Man (which bred differing styles of riding, anyway, and it was rare that habitues of one visited the other). But for the rest, potential competitors had to make do with a collection of parkland circuits which afforded gravel-path racing rather than road-racing as we know it now.

Club life in the 1930s, as exemplified by a gathering of riders at Robertsbridge, Sussex, in 1938. BSA, Vincent-HRD, Brough Superior, and Norton machines can be seen, and the occasion is probably the start of a trial

These came in two sizes, small and smaller, and none were tinier than two in the Wigan area of Lancashire. Tiniest of all was at Delph Tea Gardens, Parbold, an affair set in a quarry, but not very much bigger was the Park Hall track at Charnock Richard (adjoining the present M6 service station), where it was reputed that at least two bikes finished up in the lake at each meeting – and legend has it that there are still the remains of a couple of models beneath its weedy waters.

Another, slightly longer, Park Hall circuit was at Oswestry, on the Welsh border. In the Midlands, a few meetings were staged at Drayton Manor, Tamworth (now a pleasure park). Bradford had its

An Alexandra Palace race shot, with Tommy Wood leading W. Antell (both on 350 cc Velocettes) on the lower part of the circuit at the July, 1935, event

One of the better-known small circuits was Syston Park, near Grantham, but attendances fell gradually, leading to abandonment of the venue, once Donington Park had opened its gates. In this view we are looking from Syston Hairpin up the starting straight

Esholt Park circuit, and Manchester even held a couple of winter races in Belle Vue Gardens, with the snow-covered outdoor dance floor as the starting grid.

London was served by Crystal Palace, initially a gravel-path track but later considerably modified to provide a more acceptable tarred surface; there, stars of the magnitude of Doug Pirie, Harold Daniell, and Tommy Wood could be seen in action. Up in north London, two events were run in the grounds of Alexandra Palace, where competitors not only had to negotiate a gravelled stretch but also a road laid with tramway tracks.

Possibly the best-known provincial venue was Syston Park, near Grantham, which usually attracted a good-quality entry, even though the circuit itself left a great deal to be desired. But Syston was to lead, indirectly, to the establishment of another circuit which, in the course of the years, was to earn international fame. That circuit was Donington Park, near Derby, and the story of its founding is worth telling.

It so happened that in 1931 the Derby and District Motor Club had intended to enter a team of riders for the Manx Grand Prix and, accordingly, club secretary Fred Craner entered his prospects for the Easter meeting at Syston Park, as part of the training and selection programme. Fred had been a racer himself, until he suffered a bad crash in the 1929 Junior TT, and he was well acquainted with the Syston Park circuit and its organisers.

On this particular occasion, Fred fell out with the Syston crowd over a number of points, among them the fact that despite an advertised admission charge of 1s (5p), this had been increased to 2s 6d (12½p) without prior warning to the public. The upshot of the row was that Fred Craner swore to set up an opposition race meeting which would wipe Syston Park off the map.

It was no idle threat, and Fred began immediately to investigate the possibilities of other large estates around Derby. In due course he came to Donington Park, and saw that two of the estate roads could be linked without too much trouble, to make a useful little track. At this point, however, he was apprehended by a gamekeeper who was suspicious of Fred's activities, and was marched off to see the owner of the estate, Mr J. G. Shields.

To him, Fred explained that he was exploring the possibilities of a motor cycle racing circuit. This cut no ice with Mr Shields, who retorted that he hated motor cycles and would not have them on his estate.

'Let me run a meeting,' pleaded Fred Craner, 'and

A sport which attracted a lot of club interest in the 1930s was Moto-Ball, or motor cycle football. This is the Chester MC team, with trials rider Colin Edge (*centre*) as goalkeeper. Others are, *left*, Colin Parker and Frank Shaw and, *right*, George Milton and Jack Smith

I can almost guarantee an extra ten thousand visitors to Donington Park on a Bank Holiday.' That duly impressed Mr Shields, and he promised to think it over. The thinking-over did not take very long, because next morning he rang Fred to say that he had a deal. The linking road was put in hand immediately, and a track which, to a great extent, followed the line of today's Donington Park circuit came into being in only five weeks.

The opening meeting was held on Whit Monday, 1932, and the crowds turned up in such numbers that the gatekeepers ran out of admission tickets and had to resort to collecting money in buckets and hand basins. The temporary surface was largely of gravel, and accidents were frequent, but by the time of the next meeting, scheduled for August Bank Holiday, the whole of the two-mile lap had been tarred. One further meeting was held in 1933, an all-star event in September; faced with such formidable opposition, Syston Park closed down, as Fred Craner had predicted.

During the winter, additional amenities were put in hand, and a year later a loop was added to the west of Red Gate Lodge. Later improvements included another straight (the present finishing straight), in parallel with the original road from Coppice Corner to Red Gate and this, together with the east loop, became the Manufacturers' Circuit, used for minor club racing but, more importantly, as a testing ground for motor cycle and car makers, among them Rolls-Royce.

The ultimate extension of the pre-war Donington Park track was in 1937, when the Red Gate loop was extended over the brow of the hill and down to a hairpin turn at Melbourne Corner. Furthermore, the track was widened throughout to meet international car-racing requirements, and a new grandstand was erected to the east of Red Gate Lodge (outside the present circuit). Old Hairpin was eased, but the roadway still ran under the arches of Starkey Bridge.

In that same year, 1937, southern-based competitors were cheered by the introduction of a new circuit at Brooklands, intended to bring at least a semblance of road racing to the concrete bowl. Known as the Campbell Circuit, it cut across the infield from Railway Straight to the Finishing Straight, which it crossed and then ran alongside. From the neighbourhood of the Test Hill, the new road snaked uphill in a steep S-bend, then joined the old track at the back of Members' Hill. In all the length was $2\frac{1}{4}$ miles and, comments Vic Willoughby, who raced on it: 'Surprisingly, it did indeed have something of a road-racing feel, even though the steep climb up through what had been the Members' Enclosure was rather more like a Wall of Death!'

Later to become technical editor of *The Motor Cycle*, Vic was a typical-of-those-days enthusiastic amateur, with little money but a burning desire to go racing. It was to encourage such men that *The Motor Cycle* had instituted its annual Clubman's Day meetings at Brooklands, starting in 1932, in conjunction with the British Motor Cycle Racing Club. Thoroughly enjoyable affairs they were, too, with events for established stars interspersed with the amateur events, and with other attractions all aimed at giving the crowd a day to remember.

For that inaugural 1932 meeting BMCRC had mustered a full cast of Brooklands aces including Barry Baragwanath with his supercharged Brough-Superior outfit, Pat Driscoll, Ben Bickell, Fergus Anderson, and Eric Fernihough. In addition, there were almost 300 entries in the clubman classes, and the programme included the names of such stars of the future as Albert Moule (490 cc Norton), entered by Kidderminster MCC, and Jack Surtees (346 cc Levis), of Croydon MCC.

In unseasonably Spring-like March weather, the whole meeting worked wonderfully. To round off the day, a double car v bike challenge was scheduled, in which Les Archer and Harry Bacon, on 350 cc ohv Velocettes, were matched against Pat Driscoll and L. T. Delaney, driving 1,500 cc Lea-Francis cars. Honours were even; Les Archer beat Delaney, and Driscoll beat Bacon. Reported *The Motor Cycle*: 'The doubting Thomases have been confounded; no timid novices were involved in terrible holocausts; no nice, everyday engines melted; there were no breakdowns in the organisation.'

At that first meeting there had been a selection of outer circuit and Round-the-Mountain races of various lengths, but severe flooding of the River

Motor cycle sport takes many forms, one of which is sand-racing. In this 1934 picture from Kirkcaldy, Fife, rider A. D. Drysdale (Rudge) seems to have gone a little past the point of no return!

Wey during the early spring of 1933 weakened the foundations of the bridge by which the banked track crossed the river and, accordingly, that year's Clubman's Day had to be modified considerably. The Round-the-Mountain races were unaffected, but flying-kilometre sprints were substituted for the Outer Circuit events, and these proved to be remarkably popular. A competitor got up speed by swooping down off the Home Banking, then arrowed through a timed kilometre marked off along Railway Straight.

Jock West and Freddie Clarke featured strongly in the BMCRC members' races, and among the clubman newcomers was David Whitworth, in due course to become a star in his own right (and also, incidentally, my wartime commanding officer in the Middle East) but here playing a very minor role as a member of the Berkhamsted and District club team in the inter-club relay race.

Right through the 1930s, *The Motor Cycle* Clubman's Day at Brooklands retained its popularity, and the last of the series was staged in the early spring of 1939. One highlight of the day was a flying-kilometre speed of 112·98 mph by George Brown, on a 998 cc Vincent-HRD. Another was a solo lap by Theresa Wallach at 101·64 mph on a 348 cc Norton borrowed from Francis Beart, a feat which gained her one of BMCRC's coveted Gold Star lapel badges. Only three girls were to earn Gold

Stars in the history of the track. The other two were Florence Blenkinsop and Beatrice Shilling.

So much for the Brooklands Clubman's Day meetings (and before leaving the subject, perhaps we should note in the results of that 1939 event, one Frank Sheene taking second place in a 250 cc race on an Excelsior; yes, Barry's dad rode, too.)

Naturally, the success of the Brooklands club meets had not gone unnoticed by the rival weekly magazine, *Motor Cycling*, which in the later 1930s was being edited by former road-racer Graham Walker. To put on yet another Brooklands meeting would be too much like playing the copycat, but Graham had a still better idea, and he put it to Donington Park supremo, Fred Craner. Why not, said he, start the 1939 racing season with a real bang, by putting on a Whitsun Donington meeting under *Motor Cycling's* sponsorship?

With a spot of judicious arm-twisting, Graham could guarantee a line-up which would include Stanley Woods, Les Archer, Crasher White, Tyrell Smith, Les Graham, Cyril Hale, Johnny Lockett, Maurice Cann, Ginger Wood, Harold Daniell, and others of like calibre. And the plan went far beyond that. There would be races for genuine clubmen on genuine road-going machines plus, a real novelty, a race for machines built prior to 1931 – the first-ever vintage race, although it was not called that at the time.

The whole affair would be preceded by the astonishing spectacle of a cavalcade of factory top brass riding in convoy from Ashby-de-la-Zouch to the track (a distance of about ten miles) on bikes of

Clubmen riders take to the hallowed concrete of Brooklands, at *The Motor Cycle's* Clubman's Day meeting in April, 1939, the last of the series. It was at this meeting that George Brown (998 Vincent-HRD) established a new flying-kilometer record at 112·98 mph

their own manufacture ranging from 98 cc auto-cycles to 1,000 cc vee-twins and Square Fours.

And so it came to pass that on the misty morning of Whit Saturday, 1939, a select multitude began to assemble in the car park of the Royal Hotel, near Ashby-de-la-Zouch railway station. More than 50 manufacturers, designers, and managers had responded to the call – although *The Motor Cycle* was later to remark, rather acidly: 'It was sad, perhaps, to note the number of brand-new coats, boots, gloves, goggles, and headgear.'

On Francis-Barnetts were Gordon Francis and Eric Barnett, Edward Turner rode a Triumph Tiger 100, Arthur and Bill Butterfield had Levises, Harry Perrey (recently appointed as sales manager of New Imperial) arrived with a model of that make, Joe Craig turned up on a BSA (a surprise, but explained by the fact that he had left the Norton company when that firm abandoned its road-racing policy for 1939), Gilbert Smith – the Norton office-boy who grew up to become managing director – drove a Norton sidecar outfit; and so on down the line.

Taking part in the run, too, were Sir Malcolm and Donald Campbell, well-known motoring journalist Tommy Wisdom, and Graham Walker in person, on the Rudge with which he had won the 1928 Ulster Grand Prix. The mists were already lifting as the ten-mile parade began, and it was in almost summer sunshine that the convoy arrived at Donington Hall for their celebratory lunch.

Among the promised attractions had been a demonstration lap by Velocette's brand-new super-charged, vertical-twin works racer, nicknamed the Roarer by development engineer Harold Willis. Unhappily, it could not be made ready in time for the meeting (for that matter, it was still not properly readied by the time the TT came around, a month later, and it was destined never to take station on a starting grid).

Disappointingly, too, the crowds failed to turn up in their expected numbers, even though presentation of a coupon clipped from that week's *Motor Cycling* would have brought the admission charge down from 2s (10p) to 1s (5p). All the same, a total attendance of 6,000 was not bad and certainly, at one bob or two, the customers got full value for their money.

Record-breaking began with the first final on the card, a 250 cc scrap involving (among others) Les Graham, Les Archer, Tyrell Smith and Harold Hartley, in the winning of which Archer (New Imperial) notched a new 250 cc eight-lap record. There were other records to come, in the 350 cc event won by Arthur Wellsted (Velocette) from Peter Goodman, Harold Daniell and Crasher White, and in the 500 cc in which Daniell (Norton) put it across Johnny Lockett, Syd Barnett and Maurice Cann.

There were full-to-overflowing fields for the standard-machine clubman races in which, contrary to some lugubrious expectations, no serious damage was done either to men or machinery. But, surprisingly, only seven men came to the line for the Clubman's pre-1931 Standard-machine Race. It was possible, of course, that Graham Walker had made the conditions a little too onerous by insisting that

the machines should have full road-going equipment including lighting sets. Certainly, a Smethwick youngster by the name of Bill Boddice had spent long hours in the workshop, jury-rigging a belt-driven dynamo, especially for the race, on his ex-works 1929 350 cc New Hudson.

The other members of that Magnificent Seven were a couple of Scotts, three assorted over-head-camshaft Velocettes, and the 1926 pushrod ohv Model 18 Norton of Ian Findlay, but the field was instantly reduced to six when, as the flag dropped, one of the Velos went on strike. After little more than a lap both Scotts had disappeared (one with a seized piston, the other with a persistent misfire), leaving only four bikes still motoring. Way out in front was Bill Boddice. Earlier, during a 350 cc race, the New Hudson had cast off its primary chain, and now the precariously fitted dynamo went winging off into space, but Bill was not going to let a little thing like that worry him, and the 10-year-old machine went tramping on with undiminished vigour.

When the exhaust rocker of Jim Purnell's 1930 KTS Velocette fractured, that left just three models still circulating – and one of those was in the kind of bother that grew more dire every second. The rider was Birmingham enthusiast Ron Russell who, as the bikes were being called forward to the start, had noticed that the front tyre was soft. With no time left in which to fit a new inner tube, all he could do was pump up hard, cross his fingers, and hope.

For a while, Ron held second place behind Boddice's flying New Hudson but as the steering grew soggier and soggier, so he dropped further astern until, with just one lap remaining, he deemed it wisest to retire.

That left Bill Boddice, as the chequered flag swept down, fully half a lap clear of Ian Findlay and that spidery but much-loved Model 18 Norton, the only other machine still circulating. Dancing on air all the way to the prize-giving rostrum, young Bill stepped forward to receive the cup from Graham Walker, but his joy was shattered when Graham, instead of offering congratulations, spoke of his 'extreme disappointment'.

As Bill recalls it today: 'I could have burst into tears. It was the first piece of silverware I had ever won, and although I realised that Graham was referring to the poor entry for the race rather than to my own performance, it was a slap in the face for a youngster on the brink of a racing career.'

But at least the New Hudson factory was pleased, even though they had abandoned motor cycle manufacture six years earlier, to concentrate on Girling brake and suspension components. They actually took a full-page advertisement in the motor cycle press to announce the (rather delayed) success of their machine!

That was the one-and-only *Motor Cycling* Donington Day, because by the time Whitsun next rolled around the world was at war. The track was taken over as an Army vehicle depot, new buildings arose, and the circuit itself was to become so scarred and altered that it was almost unrecognisable. But today Donington Park is fully alive after its long sleep, awoken by the kiss of handsome prince, Tom Wheatcroft. Some day there could even be another Donington Day, but should that come to pass, then one facet of the 1939 meeting would be very, very different; the cavalcade of British manufacturers riding their own products would be a pitifully short one.

Jack Surtees (JAP), father of the world motor cycle and car racing champion of more recent times, John Surtees, crosses the tram tracks leading to Alexandra Palace. The sidecar outfit is Jack's grass-track special, with a good supply of hand-holds for the acrobatic (but unfortunately anonymous) passenger

The years of British racing dominance

Writing in a mid-1930s issue of *Motor Cycling*, a facetious columnist once defined the Isle of Man TT as 'a race to determine who has the quickest Norton'. Such was the overwhelming superiority of the Norton racing team at that particular period, that the comment was not so very far from being the absolute truth!

The figures speak for themselves. Between 1931 and 1936, Nortons not only won 11 of the 12 Junior and Senior TT races (the exception was the 1935 Senior TT, of which more later) but occupied 28 out of a possible 36 places in the first three. Nor were the victories confined to home territory, because in 1931 alone the Norton team won ten of the major Continental Grands Prix.

Of course, Norton machines had been prominent in the previous decade, latterly using the over-head-camshaft engine originated by Walter Moore and immediately recognisable by the elongated crankcase blister which shrouded the lower bevels of the camshaft drive shaft. But in 1930 Moore departed from Norton's famous Bracebridge Street factory, to take up a position with NSU of Germany (and, soon, to produce an NSU ohc engine very similar to the Norton). It appeared that the design had been Moore's personal property, and his departure meant that a new engine had to be devised.

The work was given to the brilliant young Arthur Carroll, and what came from his board was a unit demonstrably the ancestor of every ohc Norton that followed to the end of the original company's history.

However, nearly every new design requires a season to settle down, and where Nortons were concerned 1930 was that season. But the troubles they encountered were niggly little ones and, between times, the engine showed that it held tremendous potential. Meanwhile, though, the crown was vacant, and this was the Rudge-Whitworth firm's chance to step forward as claimants. Rudge, of course, were already formidable race contenders with their pent-roof, four-valve 499 cc model, Ulster Grand Prix winner in 1928 and 1929, and with several Continental successes to its credit. In a pent-roof design the inlet and exhaust valves operate in parallel pairs, but while this is expedient for manufacture, it is not necessarily productive of the best combustion chamber shape. More effective still would be a hemispherical head in which the four valves were arranged radially, although this would require a rather complicated arrangement of valve operating gear.

Nevertheless, Rudge development engineer and race-shop gaffer George Hack decided to produce a radial-valve engine for the 1930 Junior TT, with the valves worked by two pushrods and no fewer than six inter-acting rocker arms. The scheme was entirely untried. 'In fact,' recalled Rudge teamster H. G. Tyrell Smith, many years later, 'the original plan was that the works would build just one machine, which I would ride, plus a sufficient quantity of spares. Then, almost at the last minute, factory chief John Vernon Pugh decided to enter a full three-man team, with Graham Walker and Ernie Nott as the other two riders. The only way we could get the bikes built in time was to use up all the spares we had accumulated for the race. Apart from one prototype model which had covered a fair mileage, no radial-valve engine had fired, except on the test bench, before they were shipped across to the Isle of Man as virtually unknown quantities.'

Overall design responsibility was George Hack's, with detail drawing-board work by Frank Anstey (later of the Villiers factory). Hack's apprehension about racing a new engine without an adequate stock of spares seemed fully justified when, following the first morning of TT race practice, Tyrell Smith's bike was stripped for inspection. First time out, Tyrell had certainly thrown a scare ito the opposition by slicing a healthy 26 sec from the 350 cc lap record. But in the privacy of the Rudge race camp there were long faces when it was seen that both gudgeon-pin bosses of the piston had cracked. The gloom deepened further after Ernie Nott and Graham Walker had tried out their models for the first time, when it was discovered that the piston bosses of their engines were cracked, too.

On the third practice morning, George Hack gave Tyrell instructions to rip off three fast laps in succession, just to see what would happen. Again the

Top, left: possibly the most extraordinary TT picture ever taken! Approaching Quarter Bridge in the heat-wave of the 1930 Junior TT, Freddie Hicks (AJS) slid on a patch of wet tar and, trying to regain control, got into the predicament seen here

Top, right: a few seconds after the spill shown in the previous picture, Freddie Hicks has picked up his works AJS and is checking with the Quarter Bridge course marshals before continuing. It is to be hoped that the plus-fours-clad gent with his back to the photographer did not step back and crush the Box Brownie camera he had placed on the pavement!

Above: and this is the patch of wet tar which caused all the bother, with Norton team member Tim Hunt sliding nicely. Tim, too, came off but remounted to finish in 9th place in this, his first official Norton team outing

engine was stripped, but the cracks had spread no further.

'George did a lot of calculations,' said Tyrell Smith, 'and came to the conclusion that the pistons would last eight laps before disintegrating. It was a seven-lap race, of course; but you can't say it gave the riders much mental comfort!'

New pistons were fitted to all three engines before the final practice morning, and the riders were instructed to do one slow lap each – no more! – just to take off the high spots. One lap from eight left seven; and it was a seven-lap race. There would be no margin at all. Even so, Hack had more than his share of worries because in that final practice period Walker's engine seized so enthusiastically that the

con-rod bent and the cylinder barrel parted from its crankcase flange. With no other spares available, the damage had to be made good by stripping parts from the much-abused factory prototype.

The weigh-in (after which competing machines would be locked away in a marquee until just before the race began) was scheduled for 5.30 pm that same evening. Wrote Graham Walker, in a wartime issue

Below: the Ariel Square Four did not take kindly to attempts by private owners to supercharge it. This version was produced by Cambridge University MCC stalwart, Somerville Sikes, for the 1931 Senior TT, but it retired early in the race when, inevitably, the cylinder head joint blew. The Zoller vane-type blower is mounted above the gearbox

Below, right: new engines were used by AJS for the 1934 TT races. This is the 500 cc model, which had hairpin valve springs, a bronze head, and three oil pumps. New, too, was the four-speed, foot-change Burman gearbox. Tyrell Smith, Harold Daniell and George Rowley finished 7th, 9th and 12th respectively, but the team prize went to Norton, with their 1st, 2nd and 5th placings

AJS could never be left out of the reckoning in road racing, and for the 1930 Senior TT they produced this chain-driven-ohc model, in a new frame with the tubes arranged in a straight line from steering head to rear spindle. Best placings in the race were 9th and 12th, but George Rowley later won the 500 cc Brooklands Grand Prix

Opposite, top: a complete breakaway from Scott tradition was this vertical-engined 498 cc twin, evolved for the 1930 Senior TT. Details included a four-piece built-up crank housed in an Elektron crankcase with horizontally split joint. Vibration problems in practice caused the two machines to be withdrawn from the race, and development was discontinued

Opposite, centre: first appearance of a 500 cc overhead-camshaft Velocette engine was in the 1934 Senior TT. The dual seat (irreverently known as the 'Loch Ness Monster') was also a Velocette 'first'. Note the oversize fuel tank with 'elbow rest' dents in the top face. Ridden by Walter Rusk and Les Archer, the big Velocettes were placed third and fourth

Opposite, bottom: the unique 498 cc Senior TT Excelsior of 1934 featured twin magnetos and sparking plugs. Design was largely the work of Alan Bruce and the engine was of Excelsior's own manufacture. Details include a light-alloy cylinder barrel and bronze cylinder head. It was ridden by Ted Mellors but failed to finish

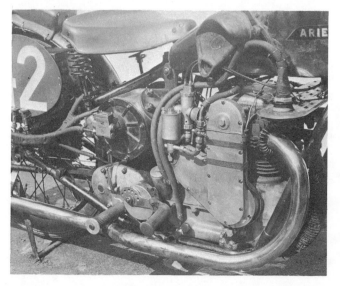

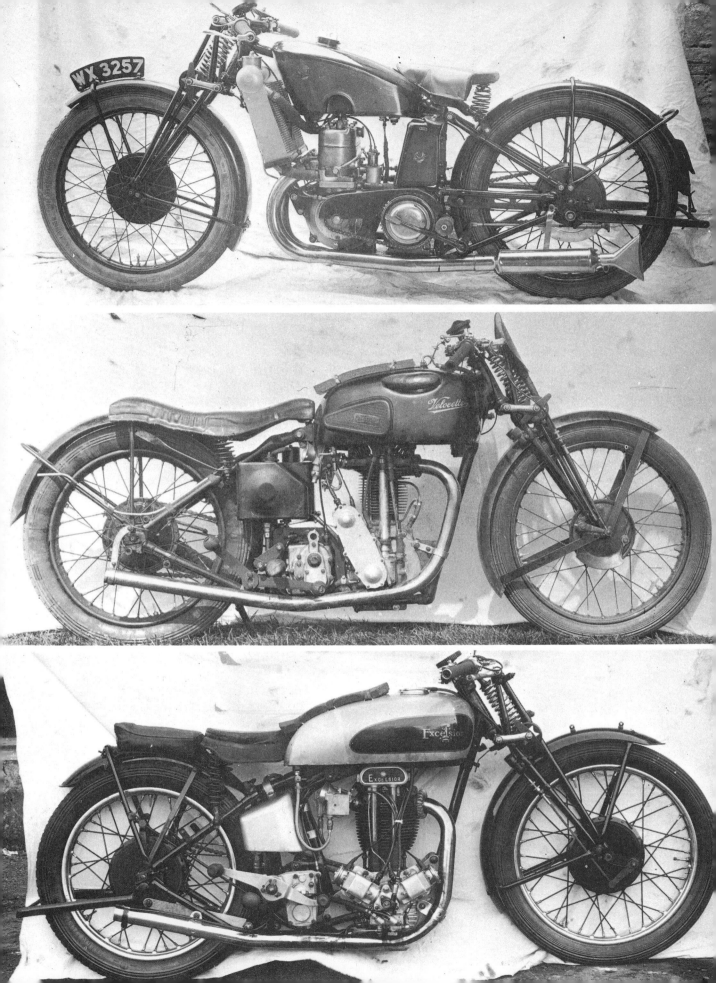

of *Motor Cycling*: 'While the others sat down to lunch I set off, fortified by a Guinness, to run to Kirkmichael and back to give everything a chance to bed in.'

At a team conference that evening, after the machines had been handed in, Graham was given special orders not to exceed half-throttle until he had passed his usual seize-up point at the top of Creg Willey's Hill, then three-quarter throttle for the rest of the lap. Tyrell's instructions were very different. 'We felt that Charlie Dodson, on the works Sunbeam, was the main threat, and so I was told to go all out from the start in the hope that Charlie would blow up in trying to keep ahead of me. That's exactly what did happen.'

Yet what if Tyrell had blown up his own engine in the process? Well, Rudge were after a race win rather than the team prize, and Ernie Nott would therefore step up into the pacemaker position. 'Another thing I remember,' recalled Tyrell, 'is that George Hack wrote down on the back of a cigarette packet the times in which, he thought, I would complete each of the seven laps. It was uncannily accurate, all the way through, only a second or so out either way. No, he didn't try to control me to those times – it was just the way things worked out!'

Of the race itself, little needs to be said. Only 3 sec astern of Charlie Dodson on the opening lap, Tyrell was dead level with him on corrected time second time around then, after the Sunbeam disappeared, he went ahead into a lead which he never lost. Nott and Walker began to enter the picture from the fourth lap and, as the last lap began, they were sitting in second and third places behind Smith. The Rudge signalling station was at Ramsey, and all three riders were given the 'hold it as you are' sign. 'It was all so uneventful, really,' said Tyrell.

Uneventful until the three Rudges were dismantled in the measuring tent, that is. There was a broken inlet-valve spring in Tyrell's engine, and a broken exhaust-valve spring in Ernie's. But, as Hack had predicted, the piston bosses of all three engines were cracked – and, in addition, Graham's piston was slit almost all the way down to the bottom of the skirt. The bike would not have travelled more than another mile!

For the same week's Senior TT, Rudge were relying on the pent-roof 500 cc engine, and at one time it looked as though they were going to make it a double 1-2-3. That was certainly the order on the fifth lap, but then Tyrell Smith started dropping back; he was using an experimental 14 mm sparking plug, and a misfire developed. Wal Handley had been due to ride a unit-construction FN in the race,

but the Belgian factory could not get it ready in time and, instead, he had opted to ride a Rudge – fortunately so, because now Wal took over the lead, to be flagged in as winner with Graham Walker second.

First-second-third in the Junior, and first-second in the Senior. In normal trading times, such an overwhelming result should have sent the demand for road-going Rudges soaring. But the world was in the grip of the deepest trade depression ever known, and there could be little hope that Rudge could recoup, in enhanced sales, the money expended on the race machines.

Nevertheless, the factory decided to go ahead, for 1931, with a 250 cc version of the radial-valve engine (they experimented, also, with a vee-twin 250 cc radial, but abandoned this). Again the team would comprise Tyrell Smith, Ernie Nott, and Graham Walker – even though the sight of 15-stone Graham trying to tuck himself away on a lightweight model made the cartoonists lick their pencil-tips with glee.

In the race, Rudge looked like pulling off a 1-2-3 once more, and that was the order as the last lap began, but leader Ernie Nott was in trouble with a tappet that kept slackening off. He carried no spanners, and had to get along as best he might by leaning down while on the move, and tightening the tappet locknut by hand. In that manner he kept going, but understandably at a slower speed. Ernie was to finish fourth, while Graham Walker was flagged in to his first and only TT success, with Tyrell Smith in second berth.

By that time the fortunes of the Rudge company were nose-diving. A team was fielded for 1932, although without the spectacular victories of the previous year, but in March, 1933, the works were in liquidation, a receiver was in occupation, and John Vernon Pugh was on a sickbed. There could be no question of a 1933 racing team – or at least, not an official one, and instead Smith, Nott, and Walker were granted permission to borrow the factory race bikes and run them, privately, under the Graham Walker Syndicate banner.

Opposite, top: the 250 cc JAP-engined Chris Tattersall Special, which finished 7th in the 1934 Lightweight TT, earning a silver replica. Average speed was 64·45 mph

Opposite, centre: trials specialist (and in post-war years Royal Enfield sales manager) Jack Booker raced this 488 cc four-valve model in the 1934 Senior TT, but came off on greasy roads on the fourth lap. Unusually, the big-end bearing was a Duralumin floating bush, forerunner of the floating bush used by Royal Enfield up to the mid-1960s

Opposite, bottom: 245 cc Dunelt-Python ridden in the 1934 Lightweight TT by T. Peeny. It finished 15th, one place ahead of Stanley Wood's (sick) Moto Guzzi

94

Strong contender for racing glory was Sweden's Husqvarna factory, and three of the works 500 cc vee-twins are seen on the starting grid of the 1935 Swedish Grand Prix at Saxtorp. Nearest the camera is the eventual winner, Stanley Woods. With No. 2 machine is Ingmar Skeppstedt, who dropped out with a puncture while in second place

Velocette had experimented in 1931 and 1932 with a supercharged overhead-camshaft single (dubbed 'Whiffling Clara' by Velo race-shop chief Harold Willis, the machine still survives in an incomplete state). As at first built, the Foxwell supercharger blew through the carburettor, but that idea did not work very well and, for 1932, a simplified arrangement was adopted in which the blower was interposed between the carburettor and the engine. Willis himself did the riding, but Clara's outings in the Junior and Senior races were doomed, for the machine retired with a broken rocker arm in the first and with a loose carburettor jet in the second.

It was back to the unblown engine, in both 350 and 500 cc versions, but the day of Velocette glory was still a few years away. Consistency, however, was something else, and in the 1933 Junior TT the machines from Hall Green finished 4th, 5th, 6th, 7th, 8th, 9th, 10th, 13th, 14th, 15th, and 16th. Back at Brooklands, Les Archer won the Hutchinson 100 at 100·61 mph, the first time the ton-hour had been recorded by a three-fifty on British soil.

, First appearance of the 500 cc racer was in 1934, when Belfast's 'Blond Bombshell', Walter Rusk, brought it into third place in the Senior TT, in the same year winning the Ulster Grand Prix with a new lap record of 92·13 mph.

For all that, Nortons occupied the very top of the tree, and for seven racing seasons the team made

Top, right: head of the Rudge range was the 499 cc Ulster, shown in 1937 form with parallel inlet and radial exhaust valves. A new feature for that year was that the pushrods ran direct on the cam followers
Right: possibly the classic engine of all time, the single-ohc 490 cc Norton International is seen here in 1934 style. Designer was Arthur Carroll, later killed in a motor cycle road accident

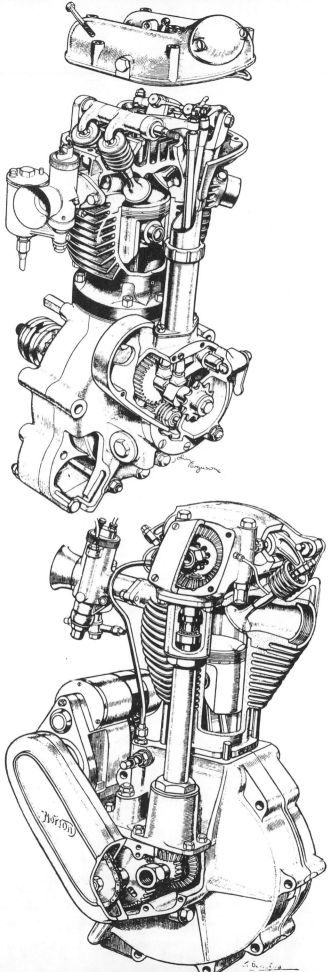

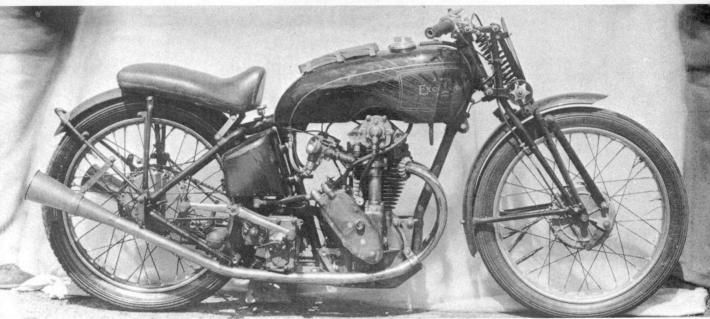

Top: impressive, but not the easiest machine to handle, Ginger Wood's New Imperial vee-twin for the 1936 Senior TT featured an all-riveted Duralumin fuel tank, and contoured racing dual seat

Above: novelty in the 1936 Lightweight TT was provided by Excelsior, with a four-valve version of the overhead-camshaft Manxman engine, fed by two Bowden (originally known as Vici) carburettors. Despite covering only one lap on the model during practice week, Tyrell Smith collected an encouraging second place, astern of Bob Foster's unit-construction New Imperial

virtually a clean sweep of every Grand Prix that offered, in both the 350 and 500 cc categories.

The engine, throughout was the Arthur Carroll design, but with improvements as one year succeed-

ed another. Aluminium-bronze cylinder heads were tried out in 1932, followed a year later by bi-metal heads in which a silicon-alloy exterior was incorporated with a bronze skull. Hairpin valve springs, megaphone exhausts and a dual ignition system were 1934 features (the second sparking plug was inserted behind the camshaft drive, and could only be reached after first removing the cambox).

It was not that a diet of continual successes had made the Norton squad complacent, but the 1935 Senior TT was to shake Bracebridge Street fans rigid. The event had been postponed for a day because of bad weather, but when the race did get under way Norton team leader Jimmy Guthrie

Third finisher in the 1938 Senior TT, Ted Mellors wheelies his works Velocette past Parkfield Corner. The machine has full oil-damped swinging-arm rear springing

moved into his customary position at the head of things, with Walter Rusk slipping into second.

This year, Stanley Woods had forsaken the vee-twin Husqvarna, to straddle a 120-degree Moto Guzzi vee-twin (equipped, incidentally, with pivoted-fork rear suspension, the springs being housed in horizontal tubes and with damping controlled by adjustable friction discs). Only a few days earlier, Stanley, with a horizontal-engine Moto Guzzi single, had won the Lightweight TT in fine style. Now, after a slow start, he overtook Walter Rusk to move into second position.

As the lap began Guthrie held a 26 sec advantage – which seemed safe enough to the Norton camp, because Jimmy had already stopped to refuel, while Stanley had yet to top up a second time. At the Moto Guzzi pit counter, the attendants made themselves look busy with the refuelling pipe; Woods, obviously, was coming in for his stop, but such was the difference in the starting order between the two men that Guthrie was away at the far side of the course and approaching his Ramsey signal station. There, he got the 'OK' board.

But the Moto Guzzi men were foxing, and Woods screamed past into his final lap with no suggestion of stopping. No time now to flash a warning to Jimmy Guthrie who, with the race seemingly safe in the bag, was climbing up the Mountain road. As the big

Moto Guzzi tore out towards the west of the island, in came Guthrie to a hero's welcome. Agreed, he had eased back the throttle a little on that final tour, but he still had plenty of time in hand, hadn't he? Hadn't he . . . ?

No, by gosh he hadn't, for Stanley Woods was riding one of his finest races, and now there came a sudden, urgent message from the Bungalow, almost the highest part of the Isle of Man course. Woods had wiped out the deficit, and at that point the two men were level-pegging – with the downhill swoop to Douglas yet to come.

Home at last came Woods, and timekeepers both amateur and official studied their watches. Stanley had done it – by 4 sec only, but the Norton stranglehold had at last been broken, and for the first time in 20 years a foreign bike had won the Senior TT. Nevertheless, for Woods it had been touch and go, because in the machine examination tent it was discovered that the fuel tank was bone dry, and the two carburettor float bowls held the odd drop or two. He would never have been able to make it to the foot of Bray Hill, had the race been longer.

But what was that mention of Woods on a Husqvarna in 1934? This was a 50-degree vee-twin designed by Folke Mannerstedt, but the Swedish manufacturers that year suffered so much bad luck, you just would not believe . . . They had made entries in both the Junior and Senior TT races, and the bikes were packed into the back of a lorry which was to be shipped to Britain; except that at Gothenburg docks one of the cables hoisting the truck and its precious cargo aloft snapped. The truck turned upside down, spilling the bikes all over the quayside and doing tremendous damage to them.

There was nothing for it but to rush the damaged models back to the works and there salvage what could be salvaged. Day and night work got some of them back into a raceworthy state, but the fates had not yet done with Husqvarna because during the TT practice period Ragnar Sunnqvist went down with appendicitis and was forbidden to ride, and Stanley Woods broke the front down tube of the five-hundred when he hit a sheep near Ballig Bridge.

In the Junior race, Ernie Nott did well to finish third behind Norton teamsters Jimmy Guthrie and Jimmy Simpson, because not only did he have a misfire but, also, oil from the timing chest was finding its way on to the rear tyre and causing some hair-raising skids. In the corresponding Senior event Stanley Woods worked into second place and rattled up a new lap record, cast himself off at Ramsey Hairpin and remounted, then ran out of fuel on the last lap within eight miles of the finish.

Above: Norton works teamster Crasher White is jerked from the saddle as his tele-forked, rear-sprung 1938 Senior TT machine hits the bump at the foot of Bray Hill. He finished fourth, helping Norton to take the team award

Above, right: better known in post-war days as a sidecar man, Eric Oliver pounds his privately owned 490 Norton down Bray Hill in the 1938 Senior TT. A split tank put him out of the race on the fifth lap

The Swedish firm did not return to the Isle of Man for the 1935 races (and maybe that is not to be wondered at!), but they did scoop up a fair share of awards elsewhere. Woods was back in a Husqvarna saddle for the Swedish Grand Prix, which he won, but the most satisfying result of all for the Swedish team came in Germany where, on the banked and super-fast Avus Ring in Berlin, Ragnar Sunnqvist finished first, ahead of the works, supercharged BMW of Karl Gall.

The Isle of Man authorities had first given financial help to the TT series in 1930, to the extent of £5,000, of which £3,500 was to encourage overseas entries by paying their expenses in part. In turn, the ACU played their part by reducing the entry fee by half in poverty-stricken 1931 (although at £16, it was still beyond the means of many a would-be racer). The same year, BBC Radio extended their coverage of the meeting, with three instead of two commentary points.

In spite of all this, 1932 entries were well down, but the presence as a spectator of the Duke of York (soon to become King George VI) did a little to bring crowds to the Island. For 1933, a revival of the Sidecar TT was proposed, and entry forms distributed, but those who had clamoured so loudly for the race backed away when asked to implement their promises. Only seven entries were received, one of them a works entry from Brough-Superior, and in consequence the event was scrubbed from the programme. As part of a job-providing scheme, the Isle of Man Highways Board fenced the whole of the Mountain section of the course, at a total cost of £79,000.

For several years, *Motor Cycling* had been organising a day excursion to the Senior TT (a practice still carried on by that magazine's successor, *Motor Cycle Weekly*), and as a nostalgic flashback it might be worth mentioning that the 1934 trip would have cost a participant just £1 12s 6d (£1·62½p), which included rail fare from his nearest station, the boat trip, two suppers, and breakfast at Cunningham's Young Men's Holiday Camp. And do not say *that* was not value for money!

Continental challenge

With no Rudge works team for 1933, especially in the 250 cc class, this led to a brief battle for road-racing supremacy between two more British contenders, New Imperial and Excelsior. Both had been prominent at home and abroad since the mid-1920s, New Imps with straightforward pushrod overhead-valve engines of their own manufacture, and Excelsior (known in some countries as Bayliss-Thomas, to avoid confusion with the American Excelsior company) with JAP-engined models of 175 cc and 250 cc raced by the Crabtree brothers, Syd Gleave, Eric Fernihough and, at Brooklands, Chris Staniland.

Most successful of the New Imperial riders of the time were Ted Mellors, Leo Davenport, and Les Archer who, with a part-faired New Imp, made the first 100 mph lap of Brooklands by a 250 cc machine

New Imperial had recently moved to their newly-erected home at Spring Road, Hall Green, Birmingham when this picture of Leo Davenport and the 1931 250 cc TT model was taken outside the brand-new office door. An interesting feature was that in order to cool the oil, the return line to the oil tank passed through the petrol tank. Leo got no further than Quarter Bridge on the first lap before being eliminated by plug trouble, but won the race for New Imperial next year

– in so doing, snatching the lap record from Excelsior-mounted Monty Saunders.

It had been a good 1932 season for New Imperial, with 1-2-3 wins in the Belgian and Dutch Grands Prix, and 1933 began well with Ted Mellors again winning the Dutch and claiming second spot in the Belgian. But the Isle of Man TT was one event which really counted, and there the New Imp camp came up against a brand-new Excelsior secret weapon, devised by Ike Hatch of the Blackburne factory, and Eric Walker of Excelsior. This was a radial-head four-valver, the overhead gear of which was so complex that the model was to earn the nickname of the Mechanical Marvel.

At that time Excelsior's had no engine manufacturing facilities of their own, and so the Mechanical Marvel unit was specially built for them at the Blackburne works at Great Bookham, Surrey. It had two independent camshafts – inlet across the rear, exhaust across the front, and the pushrods operated sliding members which, in turn, worked the rocker arms. A very modern specification included Elektron crankcases, and forged connecting rod and piston in Hiduminium light-alloy. A needle-roller big end bearing, and a BTH magneto driven by skew gearing and lying alongside the crankcase were other changes to standard design practice.

For the 1933 Lightweight TT, the Excelsior camp pinned their hopes on Syd Gleave and Wal Handley, and although a scintillating performance by a machine straight off the drawing-board may have seemed too much to hope for, the fact remained that as the opening lap ended Handley was the undoubted leader – and Gleave lay second, only 1 sec astern.

That was the way it stood, right to the last lap when Handley's engine packed up at Sulby, with less than 20 miles of the race left to run. But Gleave kept going, to come home winner with Charlie Dodson, of the rival New Imperial outfit, as runner-up. That, however, was to be the Mechanical Marvel's only major victory, and the following year Gleave could manage no higher than sixth in the event. Nor did New Imperial do much better and, instead, the 1934 Lightweight TT proved to be yet another 1-2-3 for

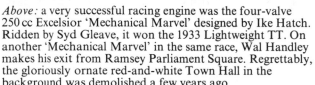

Above: a very successful racing engine was the four-valve 250 cc Excelsior 'Mechanical Marvel' designed by Ike Hatch. Ridden by Syd Gleave, it won the 1933 Lightweight TT. On another 'Mechanical Marvel' in the same race, Wal Handley makes his exit from Ramsey Parliament Square. Regrettably, the gloriously ornate red-and-white Town Hall in the background was demolished a few years ago

Top, right: although the Excelsior Manxman never won a TT ace, this solidly-built overhead-camshaft unit had a well-deserved reputation for racing reliability. Seen here is the racer's sports-roadster cousin, the 248 cc Manxman of 1937, with Lucas Magdyno electrics

Above: the Mechanical Marvel', though successful, was too finicky to be adapted as a production model, and in its place Excelsior devised an ohc model with shaft and bevel camshaft drive. This was the rightly famed Excelsior Manxman, and the picture shows a 1935 350 cc model, restored by Sammy Miller

the Rudges, now running as a private squad – the Graham Walker Syndicate.

Incidentally, that race was to provide 'machine breaker' Jimmy Simpson, so often a non-finisher yet so often the maker of the fastest lap, with his sole TT win. At last Unlucky Jim could bow out of the racing picture a happy man. On the second Rudge was Ernie Nott, and third was Graham Walker, who, like Simpson, was in his last racing season.

Fast though the Mechanical Marvel was, it was finicky to keep in tune, and the Excelsior company decided to evolve another and simpler type of engine. Again Ike Hatch and Eric Walker were

responsible, and the result of their work was the Manxman, one of the most handsome racing motor cycles (and there were to be sports-roadster versions, too) ever manufactured. The power unit was a classic two-valve overhead-camshaft job, the camshaft being driven by a vertical shaft and bevels, as in the Norton and Velocette.

Made in both 250 cc and 350 cc capacities (the works also raced a 500 cc, although this was never sold to the public) the Manxman failed to hit the heights, either in two-valve form or in the four-valve variety raced in 1936, although Ginger Wood's 80·65 mph second place in the 1936 Ulster Grand Prix was the only occasion on which a British two-fifty finished the Clady Circuit at an over-80 mph average speed.

What the Manxman did gain was a wholesome reputation for reliability, that made it a prime favourite among private entries. To illustrate the point, the 1938 Lightweight TT was won by Germany's Ewald Kluge on one of the exotic supercharged DKW two-strokes – but Excelsiors were 2nd, 3rd, 4th, 5th, 6th, 7th, 9th and 13th, and one can hardly find anything more reliable than that.

New Imperial, too, had a new bike for the 1935 season. From 1932 the company had been building a very successful range of unit-construction singles for the everyday public, and now Matt Wright (who in post-war days was to be associated with the AJS 7R Boy Racer, together with the ubiquitous Ike Hatch) produced a unit-construction pushrod 250 cc, with the lower part of the engine, and the gearbox internals, housed in one big magnesium-alloy casting. The assembly was not as oiltight as it could have been, and in consequence Bob Foster, its rider, dubbed it the Flying Pig Trough.

That first year, a number of bugs had to be shaken out of the design, but in 1936 Foster won the Lightweight TT at a new record average of 74·28 mph. It was touch and go, though. During the practice period, the New Imp's oil consumption had been prodigious, and as the race ran into its closing stages an agonising decision had to be taken in the New Imperial pit. Should Bob be called in at the end of the penultimate lap, for an oil top-up? That was the prudent course, but it would have had the disadvantage of robbing him of precious seconds.

'No,' said New Imperial's founder and managing director, Norman Downs, 'wave him on and keep your fingers crossed.' The decision was the right one, and Bob Foster cracked round the final lap to give Britain its last-ever 250 cc victory. It was, also, the last time a pushrod overhead-valve engine would win a solo Isle of Man TT (Clubman's races

Below: the vertical-engine 246 cc OK Supreme engine designed by George H. Jones and Ray Mason was first seen in 1934, but for the 1936 Lightweight TT a redesigned mechanism with hairpin valve springs was evolved by Pat McIver; unfortunately OK Supreme boss Ernie Humphries refused to pay royalties and so for the race, in which the all-white bike was to be ridden by USA stunt rider Putt Mossman (in all-white leathers) a return was made to coil springs. It was all in vain, anyway, because Putt turned up late, and failed to qualify

Below, right: last British-built machine to win the 250 cc Lightweight TT was the unit-construction New Imperial, ridden by Bob Foster in 1936. Bob gave the bike the nickname of 'The Flying Pig Trough' because, he said, it slurped its way through so much oil

Opposite, top: the Husqvarna works 500 cc twin as raced by Stanley Woods and Ernie Nott in the 1934 Senior TT. Woods ran out of petrol on the last lap while running second. Nott retired on the first lap with gearbox trouble

Opposite, centre: sensation of the 1936 racing scene was Velocette's new rear-sprung frame, employing oil-damped air spring units. After a try-out in the Swiss Grand Prix, Stanley Woods took this 499 cc model to second place (behind Jimmy Guthrie's Norton), in the Senior TT

Opposite, bottom: Norton's first rear-sprung racing model was a spring-heel type. Both Junior and Senior models were built, and the picture shows the 499 cc version (the first year that engine capacity had been increased from 490 cc) for the 1936 Senior TT. Other new features were a light-alloy barrel and head with increased fin area, and a twin-spark magneto

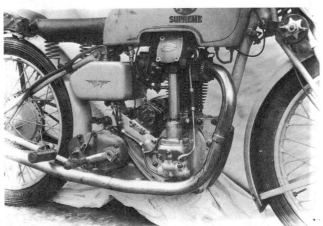

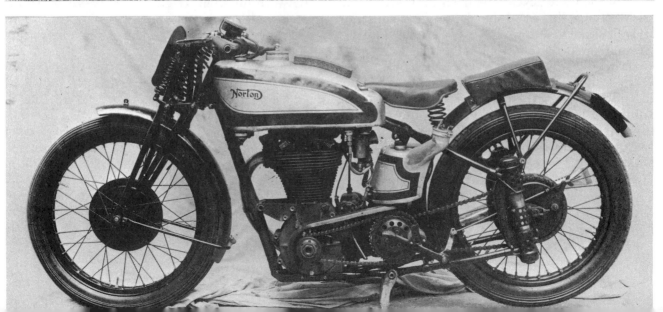

Possibly the most successful – and certainly the most audible – 250 cc racing bike of the later 1930s was the DKW. Ernie Thomas is seen winning the 1937 250 cc class Ulster Grand Prix at a record 81·83 mph

excepted). Later the same year, New Imp fanciers had more cause to cheer when Ginger Wood and Bob Foster brought off a 1-2 victory in the 250 cc section of the Ulster Grand Prix; Bob's bike was the TT winner (at the time of writing, the sole souvenir of this machine is a half-crankcase hanging on a wall of Taylor's Garages in Shipston on Stour), but Ginger rode an earlier non-unit-construction model.

To some degree a parallel can be drawn between the fortunes of New Imperial and Rudge, because each was headed by a man who had been responsible for the motor cycle side from the start; in the case of Rudge this was John Vernon Pugh, and his equivalent at New Imperial was Norman Downs, who had founded the marque in the early 1900s after acquiring the moribund Hearl and Tonks cycle works. Rudge started to slide at about the same time that John Pugh fell ill. And now the illness of Norman Downs coincided with a downturn in New Imperial finances. Indeed, in Mr Downs's absence his fellow directors had closed down the racing shop and distributed its personnel elsewhere throughout the factory. Paying a visit to the plant during a part-recovery of health, he discovered this and gave immediate orders for the race programme to be reinstated. It was as a result of this personal intervention that work on the racing vee-twin, and

on the bike that was to win the 1936 Lightweight TT, recommenced.

However, the big difference between Rudge and New Imperial was that while the money troubles of the former were caused by a fall in orders, New Imp's difficulties came from a totally opposite reason. They were just *too* successful; in picking up sales, and finding the orders rather too many for their Hall Green works to handle, they resorted to farming-out work to sub-contractors. Inevitably (as had happened with Douglas, when they adopted the same practice in 1927) the bought-out work proved to be less reliable than their own, and the company became involved in a large amount of unprofitable rectification, to honour customer guarantees.

Between the Lightweight TT successes of Rudge in 1934 and New Imperial in 1936, an intruder had broken in. As mentioned in the previous section, 1935 brought the Lightweight TT title to the horizontal-engined 250 cc single Moto Guzzi ridden by Stanley Woods. This horizontal two-fifty had been a threat ever since 1926 when Pietro Ghersi, second finisher in the Lightweight TT, was disqualified for having committed the terrible crime of using a different make of sparking plug than that specified on his weighing-in sheet. Revenge had been a long time coming, but now Woods provided it in double measure by giving Moto Guzzi their second TT win of the week in the Senior with a wide-angle vee-twin.

Meanwhile, back in Bracebridge Street, Norton's race supremo Joe Craig continued to wreak his

annual miracle of squeezing just enough extra power from the good old overhead-camshaft single to keep it nicely and reliably ahead of the pack, although by this time Velocette were coming more and more into the picture. Not even Woods's Senior TT win would convince Craig of the superiority of a multi-cylinder engine, and the 114·09 mph reached at Montlhéry by Jimmy Guthrie on a dope-burning 500 cc Norton prepared in the racing shop, seemed reasonable confirmation of his views.

Pursuing a totally different policy, DKW produced a new 500 cc two-stroke for the 1935 German Grand Prix with no fewer than five pistons, the explanation being that it was a double split-single, with an additional supercharging cylinder. Particular attention had been paid to weight-saving, and the machine was even equipped with a light-alloy exhaust system.

'One no longer says Good Morning in Germany,' observed a British reporter at that meeting, noting the hands constantly raised in salute. 'Everywhere there are Nazi swastikas. Everybody seems to be somebody important.'

But if the Germans were praying for a home victory, their prayers went unanswered. Nortons were at full strength, the DKW failed to last the course, and the 500 cc victor was Guthrie, leading home Swedish ace Ragnar Sunqvist on his Husqvarna vee-twin.

The same year saw the advent of a new and revolutionary Italian machine, built by a Rome concern. Its co-designer was Piero Taruffi, and its name was the Rondine – an across-the-frame four-cylinder with a supercharger and water-cooling. It was not yet ready for international competition, but in December, 1935 it gave a hint of things to come when Taruffi himself covered the flying kilometre at 151·84 mph, a handsome improvement on the record previously standing to the credit of Ernst Henne's BMW.

The following year the Rondine design was bought by Gilera. Taruffi's services went with the deal and he, and Gilera's Ing Pietro Remor, began to develop the machine for road racing. Road tax concessions had given the 175 cc class a strong following among Italy's road-going motor cyclists, and this in turn fostered 175 cc racing at club and national level and the growth of the typical Italian double-ohc single with its camshafts driven by a train of gears. A prominent producer of this type of machine was Benelli, and it was no real surprise to see Benelli stepping up to the international 250 cc class by 1936.

That year's German Grand Prix saw the introduc-tion of ready-steady-go colour-light starting. More than 240,000 enthusiasts paid admission to the Nürburgring circuit, hoping that DKW would fare better this time. And so they might have done, had not there been a thorough shambles in the pits. Out in front in the 500 cc race was Jimmy Guthrie and his Norton, but the DKWs of Otto Steinbach and Hans-Peter Müller were lying second and third. Both DKW men pulled into the pits at the same time, Steinbach opened the radiator filler cap of his water-cooled two-stroke and received a face-full of steam which caused him to drop the bike, knocking over Müller's model in the panic.

Frith won the 350 cc event for Norton, and after a brave fight Tyrell Smith brought the Excelsior home ahead of the DKW and Benelli men.

Velocette tried the effect of a double-ohc valve arrangement in 1936, although rather unsuccessfully, the Norton camp meanwhile were juggling with bore and stroke dimensions to evolve a 499 (instead of 490 cc) engine and a new frame with plunger-type rear suspension. Notwithstanding the Velocette experience, Norton's, too, designed a double-knocker which was widely publicised in the technical press, and took it to the Isle of Man in 1937.

Indeed, the race reports of the time were unanimous in saying that the new Norton engine, campaigned by Freddie Frith, had won the Senior race. Not until many years later did the truth emerge, that the double-knocker had given trouble during the practice period and, for the race, a single-ohc unit was substituted.

That 1937 Senior TT was quite something, because there were others with their eyes on the massive trophy, not least Velocette, who had signed Stanley Woods for the occasion, riding a model with a massive square-finned cylinder head and the oleo-pneumatic pivoted fork rear springing system introduced the previous year. Then, too, there was a first-time entry by Germany's famous BMW factory; their supercharged flat-twins, which by 1935 had already adopted double overhead camshafts and the world's first hydraulically damped telescopic front fork, had been gaining ground in continental races in the hands of Otto Ley and Karl Gall. For the Isle of Man, where the $37\frac{3}{4}$-mile circuit could not readily be learned in one visit, BMW played safe by hiring a British rider, the brilliant Jock West.

It would seem that Joe Craig's plan was for Jimmy Guthrie to be the sacrificial goat on this occasion, his role being to go all out from the start in the hope that Stanley Woods would be tempted to give chase and, in so doing, blow up his motor. Should Guthrie's

engine blow instead – well, too bad, but there would be other Norton men hanging around on the fringe of the scrap, ready to take over.

And that was exactly what happened. Guthrie retired with his stricken Norton at a section of the climb up from Ramsey known, at that time, as The Cutting. Freddie Frith accelerated to make up for the loss of the team leader, making the race's first-ever over-90 mph lap, to enter the final lap level-pegging with Woods. In the meantime West on the BMW, at one time in fourth place, and Omobono Tenni on the Moto Guzzi wide-angle twin, at one time fifth, were out of the running. West's fuel tank had split, but he kept going, eventually finishing sixth; Tenni, with a broken throttle cable, stopped altogether. First across the line, Frith had an agonising wait until Woods was at last flagged in; but this time Woods had not worked a miracle and it was Freddie's race – by just 14 sec.

In Britain, 1937 was Coronation Year, and to mark the crowning of King George VI, almost every little trial, grass-track, or club sports day was

Opposite, top: supercharging a single is a tricky problem, but various firms have tried out the idea. This is the Vincent-HRD Senior TT entry of 1936, but the practice period produced so many headaches that, for the race, a conventional unblown model was substituted

Opposite, lower: most exotic piece of racing machinery ever built in Britain was the supercharged vee-four AJS, initially raced in air-cooled form, but subsequently given water cooling. In essence it comprised four overhead-camshaft AJS singles on a common crankcase. This is the 1936 version

designated the Coronation Something-or-other. In the grounds of the Crystal Palace in South London, the old and twisty path-race circuit had been replaced by a much more worth-while tarmac track, and the inevitable Coronation Grand Prix opening meeting was a star-studded affair, the field including Maurice Cann, Harold Daniell, George Rowley, Charlie Manders, Ken Bills, Stanley Woods, Jock West, and Dave Whitworth.

About this time, racing development engineer Matt Wright said farewell to New Imperial and travelled south to the Associated Motor Cycles factory at Plumstead. There, his first task was the design and manufacture of a new duplex frame for

In the 1936 Senior TT, George Rowley takes the blown vee-four AJS around Ramsey Hairpin, but he is destined to retire halfway through the race

the chain-driven-ohc 350 cc AJS, an engine which had been out of the awards list for several years, although there had been steady progress in design and weight-saving (the 1935 Junior TT works models, using Elektron magnesium-alloy crankcase and gearbox castings, weighed only 270 lb).

However, the 350 cc single – forerunner of the well-loved 7R of post-war days – was rather overshadowed by a machine which was certainly the most complex racer ever built by a British company. This was the blown overhead-camshaft vee-four, in essence four chain-driven ohc singles on a common crankcase. The prototype, unblown and ostensibly a super-sports roadster, had created a sensation when it appeared on the AJS stand at the 1935 Olympia Show. At that time it was air-cooled, and it remained so when raced, in blown trim by George Rowley and Harold Daniell in the 1936 Senior TT. Both retired, and the model was withdrawn, not to re-appear on the racing scene until 1938 (this time equipped with water cooling.

That, though, is taking us a little ahead of the story, and it is time we looked at happenings in Italy where by 1937 the Rondine design had been bought by Gilera, and it was under that name that the water-cooled four took its place on the starting line

First factory to employ an oil-damped telescopic form was BMW. A Creg-ny-Baa picture showing the supercharger in front of the engine of George Meier's 1939 Senior TT winner

of the Swiss Grand Prix at Berne, ridden by its designer, Piero Taruffi, and by Giordano Aldrighetti.

Interestingly, the same race saw the surprise entry of a *diesel*-engined machine, the Stewit, ridden by Walter Hess; however, it did not figure anywhere in the results.

The Gilera demonstrated tremendous potential, but at this stage in its development it was too unreliable to be successful. On the other hand, the flat-twin BMW had become a real menace and at the Dutch Grand Prix, a fortnight after the 1937 TT meeting, Karl Gall and Otto Ley combined to put pressure on Jimmy Guthrie, the Norton ace, to such effect that the Norton blew up and Jimmy retired – a reversal of the situation of the year before, where the Norton team had ganged up on the Bee-Ems with like result.

With Guthrie out, Harold Daniell did his noble best for the Norton side but it was not quite enough, and Gall gained the winner's laurels. British honour was retrieved to some degree by first and second places to Velocette in the 350 cc class, but Tyrell Smith's works Excelsior Manxman was relegated to second place in the 250 cc class by Walfried

Winkler's thirsty, noisy, but extremely fast DKW.

DKW had another ace up their sleeve in the shape of a rotary-valve two-fifty, given an initial outing in the Belgian Grand Prix by Ewald Kluge. A fortnight later the German Grand Prix was held over the Sachsenring near Chemnitz (now Karl-Marx-Stadt) and for Britain it was to bring stark tragedy.

The 500 cc race had begun as a renewal of the Guthrie-Gall-Ley dogfight, but Ley soon dropped out of the battle with clutch trouble. After ten laps Guthrie led Karl Gall by 5 sec, but that had stretched to 85 sec at half distance, and to a commanding 92 sec with ten laps remaining. For Jimmy Guthrie, the race looked to be in the bag, but with just one mile to the finishing flag, the Norton's connecting rod snapped and Guthrie was flung against a tree and killed.

Back home, a fund was started which was to lead, in due course, to the erection of a simple stone column beside the mountain road where he had retired in his last Isle of Man race. It is, of course, the now world-famous Guthrie Memorial, a viewpoint from which visitors can enjoy the spectacular panorama of the northern plain and, beyond in the haze, the hills of Jimmy's native Scotland.

The French GP of 1937 saw a boost to Velocette morale with a double victory in the 350 cc and 500 cc classes by Ted Mellors – although it has to be said that the BMWs were not competing. Traditional nursery of Britain's road racers, the September-time Manx Grand Prix could boast of record entries, the fields of 61 Senior and 77 Junior competitors including the names of Maurice Cann, Ken Bills, Johnnie Lockett, Stan and Roland Pike, Albert Moule, Arthur Wheeler, and many more who would soon be making their marks on a wider canvas.

And so to the Ulster Grand Prix, with Jock West (BMW), Ted Mellors (Velocette) and Ernie Thomas (DKW) as respective winners of the 500, 350, and 250 cc classes. Norton had withdrawn, as a mark of respect for Guthrie. This was Jock's first win in an international road race, and the first time a foreign machine had won in Northern Ireland.

It had been a season which marked the beginning of the end of British dominance in the 500 cc class, for although Nortons had won more races than any other make the opposition had grown considerably tougher, and from now on wins would be harder-fought – and noticeably fewer. Velocette, however, were keeping the Union Jack flying in the 350 cc section, with four victories in classic events; but DKW were drawing away from the rest of the field in 250 cc racing, with five 1937 successes, to the two apiece by Moto Guzzi and Excelsior.

Mud, glorious mud

It was inevitable that the earliest manufacturers should want to demonstrate the superiority of their own particular products in competition with those of their rivals, so we can say that 'trials' have been with us since Edwardian times. Nevertheless, the nature of the sport has altered considerably over the years.

At first, the main idea was to finish, come what may. Gradually, however, penalties began to be introduced for stopping (perhaps to replace a stretched exhaust valve, or to shorten a stretched driving belt) and later as engines became more reliable, for individual performances on selected hills on the chosen route; Dashwood, the main-road climb out of West Wycombe in the Oxford direction was a favourite test hill of the 1900s, as also were Warmington and Sunrising in the Midlands.

But as time went by, so trials organisers began to run out of main-road, and even minor-lane hills stiff enough to test the performance of a motor cycle. More and more, off-road hazards such as woodland climbs, watersplashes, and deep mud crept into the routes, and the emphasis switched from machine ability to rider ability. For some while yet, makers would trumpet their trials successes in the motor cycle magazines, with the implication that bikes that would stand up to trials punishment would serve the everyday customer in like manner.

After all, trials machines – catalogued as such in maker's lists – were as yet unknown, and until well in the 1920s the competing bikes were standard models, altered but slightly to suit the individual rider's tastes. For the riders themselves it was bonanza time, with bonus money to be had from the machine and accessory makers for trials successes.

Right, top: driving the only 350 cc sidecar outfit in the 1930 Scottish Six Days Trial, Phil Cranmore (BSA), from Birmingham, tackles Falls Hill. He gained a silver cup after making best sidecar performance on every hill on the route

Right: second-day traffic jam on Mamore in the 1930 Scottish Six Days Trial. Leading rider is silver cup winner Vic Anstice (348 cc Douglas), but Alec Downie (348 cc AJS) is dismounted and pushing, while Arthur Tyler (498 cc James) seems to have given up altogether. Downie won the George Albert Trophy for 'pluck, endurance, and hard luck'; a real veteran, he had competed in the first Scottish trial in 1909

Headed by British ISDT organiser Harry P. Baughan, the Stroud-built Baughan was usually Blackburne-powered, but this 1933 348 cc Model O features a Sturmey Archer engine. Oddly, the Baughan tank badge portrayed Mercury holding a model *car*, the reason being that the factory had originally built cyclecars before turning to motor cycles

All this, though, was about to change, and the 1930s can be considered as the decade during which trials started to take on the form in which we now know the sport. It was a time during which star riders became better known – in some cases, anyway – than the machines they rode. However, there were other men who became almost synonymous with

At Peth Foot Splash, in the Travers Trophy Trial of 1934, D. Miller (BSA) takes a rather incautious line, while D. Lamb (OK Supreme) looks on in astonishment

their mounts; like Allan Jefferies and Triumph, Jack Williams and Norton, and Bert Perrigo and BSA.

Indeed, it is Bert Perrigo who now gives us a first-hand account of the trials-riding 1930s. Already a star as the decade began, he took over BSA development and team-management duties as his own trials career tailed off.

'When I began in the early 1920s,' says Bert, 'we took a standard machine and maybe modified the handlebar and footrest positions slightly, but that was about all. We didn't even have special tyres at that time, but ran on ordinary road treads, and it was not until the end of the 1920s, or the early 1930s, that anything in the nature of a competition tyre was developed.

'Then, however, we jumped in at the deep end by fitting what today would be called moto-cross treads, and with the coming of knobblies the organisers had to look for tougher and still tougher hills. The more freakish the going, the more the riders tried to compensate, and so we ended up with big, chunky four-inch knobblies that took us up the hills as though we had cog drive, and it was all getting out of hand.

'It was getting out of hand in another sense, too, because the factories were finding trials support too costly. And so in 1930 the manufacturers had a

conference, and it was decided that there would be just twelve major trials in the year that would have manufacturers' support. Successes in the selected dozen trade-supported events could be advertised, but not successes in other non-trade-supported trials. We at BSA were largely responsible for bringing in the restriction, mainly because we had so many riders on our own books, apart from others in various areas who were receiving a measure of support.

'For example, at that time the south-western area was the biggest market for motor cycles in the country, and so we kept the BSA banner flying by recruiting local riders of promise, like Mike Riley. The idea was that we would provide the machines, and we would tell them "Okay, ride in the national events and we will enter you – but we expect you also to ride in trials in your own area, paying your own way". Of course, we maintained the machines and updated them as necessary.

'All the same, as the depression hit there was a period when makers dropped trade support of trials altogether. In 1931 Graham Goodman organised the Victory Trial, and obtained money to pay riders cash bonuses by going outside the motor cycle industry as such. Things were pretty tight, but Graham got dealers, and other interested folk, to chip into a fund. Stuart Waycott, with a Rudge outfit, won the Victory Cup itself, and I won the Cranford Bowl for the best solo performance. I know that I collected £30 in bonus money, and £30 was a lot of money in those days.

'The 1932 Blue Star Competitions, based on the bike I rode myself, had upswept pipes – not that we were first, because I know Levis used upswept pipes, and so did New Imperial, I think – and as older readers will know, they suddenly became fashionable on road models, too, much to the dismay of pillion girls. The purpose of the upswept pipe was not so much to carry the exhaust clear of deep water or mud, as to narrow the bike at its lowest point, the better to negotiate ruts. For the same reason we raised the footrests a little – though not by too much, because when a trials rider takes his weight off the saddle and stands on the rests he is in fact lowering the centre of gravity of the bike.

'Not that we used to stand on the rests the way that present-day trials men do, nor did we reduce the width of the rests by very much, because remember that the majority of us rode in waders. Not until a while later, when things began to get more serious, did I take to wearing boots; they were better, of course, because they didn't slip on the footrests which, accordingly, could now be shortened. The

In the Easter sunshine, R. W. Hole takes his water-cooled 172 cc SOS up Beggars Roost in the 1935 Lands End Trial; he gained a first-class award

Higher and yet higher! To mark the 1935 official opening of the Gross Glockner Pass, the Austrian authorities organised what must have been one of the longest hill-climbs of all time

A happy bunch of trials riders snapped at the start of a Scottish Two-Days Trial, possibly in 1936. The overhead-valve Levis was especially popular as a trials machine in Scotland, and on such a model Bill Smith became Scottish trials champion

other main item of apparel was the long rubberised coat, which I always wore. This wasn't so that observers couldn't see when I dropped a foot, but simply because the Barbour type of suit was only just coming in and had yet to gain universal popularity.

'I rarely stood up on the rests when tackling a section and, instead, would poise with my bottom just hovering above the saddle. That way, I could move the bike about between my legs without transferring body weight. Jack Williams had a similar riding style to mine, as also did Allan Jefferies, and if a section called for speed, then all three of us would indulge in full-blooded charges. But Vic Brittain was totally different, a brilliant rider but a firm believer in a slow, plonking climb.

'Fred Povey was probably the instigator of the body-lean style – he and Ted Breffitt, perhaps. They would push the bike right over so far that they would be almost riding alongside, the same way that many trials riders do today.

'One of the most remarkable trials episodes of the 1930s was Allan Jefferies' win in the 1938 British Experts Trial on a side-valve Triumph. It was totally unexpected, and I'm sure he only did it for a lark, but the funny thing is that so many riders suddenly wanted to have side-valve competitions Triumphs that the factory had to build a batch, almost in self-defence! A detuned or soft-tuned engine was more controllable in trials work than a hot-stuff model. Carburation was the key, and once that was right there was no reason why a side-valve shouldn't perform just as well as an overhead-valve.

'It was towards the end of the 1930s that a lot of agitation began over the use of knobbly tyres in trials. Genuine trials machines were starting to appear in makers' catalogues, and organisers were having to include hills that were so freakish as to be dangerous. And so the ACU held a conference, or rather several conferences, at which riders and organisers could have their say. Many riders wanted to stay with moto-cross treads, having got used to them, but quite a large body of opinion was in favour of reverting to nominally standard tyres.

Biggest machine in the 1938 AJS range was the 990 cc vee-twin Model 38/2. Home or export versions were on offer, each at £84 3s. This is the home model, the export bike being fitted with foot clutch, hand gearing, footboards, and swept-back handlebars

Like flies on a flypaper, competitors struggle and fall on Red
Road Hill, Bagshot Heath, during a Bayswater MCC
scramble in June, 1937

'Possibly the first national trial to include a
"standard tyres only" clause was the 1935 Colmore
Cup. It passed off successfully, but not until 1938 did
every major trial go "standard tyre". The change
certainly made the job of the clerk of the course less
difficult, because now it was possible to bring back
one-time favourite hills that had been abandoned as
being too easy.

'The other major change was in riding technique,
because now we had to go a little quicker because of
the lack of wheelgrip, and the plonk merchants were
at something of a disadvantage. But it didn't take the
tyre manufacturers long to sense a demand, and very
soon there were special trials covers on the market,
with tread patterns that complied with the dimensions laid down by the ACU but which, at the same
time, gave us back some of the grip we had lost in the
switch-over from knobblies.

'So far I have said nothing about sidecar trials, but
we had our ace sidecar men then, as now, with
Dennis Mansell and his overhead-camshaft Norton,
the man everybody had to beat. One answer was the
two-wheel-drive outfit, and the Baughan company –
almost certainly the first in Britain to build nothing

but competitions bikes – actually catalogued a
model in which the sidecar wheel could be driven, in
addition to the machine's rear wheel, by engaging a
dog clutch. Bill Hayward won a number of major
events, while in the Midlands Ralph Dee and his
Baughan took a lot of catching, but after a while
some clubs put a ban on sidecar drive; but that was
not until other drivers had attempted to copy the
Baughan scheme. There was Howard Uzzell, who
built a BSA version – and Mansell himself, who got
Baughan's to adapt their drive to a Norton.

'Baughan's tried to get the British Army interested in the idea, and it did eventually result in the
Norton factory supplying a batch of 633 cc sidecar-
wheel-drive outfits to the Army, though I don't
think they ever saw action.'

In fact, the Belgian-based FN firm showed more
interest from a military viewpoint, and in 1939 a
batch of sidecar-wheel-drive FN outfits, built to
Baughan patents, were supplied to the Belgian
Army. When, after the outbreak of the Second
World War, Belgium was overrun by German
troops, the military FN outfits were pressed into
German Army service, and it was after a study of
these that BMW and Zündapp produced their own
sidecar-wheel-drive outfits, which were to see service
from Russia to the African desert.

Edward Turner's trendsetters

Just occasionally, folk lore turns out to have a basis of truth, and that is certainly so in the story of the Ariel Square Four. Edward Turner came from London (so the story runs) with the germ of an idea sketched on the back of a cigarette packet, his intention being to hawk it around the Midland factories until he found a buyer for the idea. Fiction? Not so, for Turner was later to reveal that that was just what did happen – adding that it was a *Wild Woodbine* cigarette packet, he not being able to afford any classier smoke.

The main problems with installing a four-cylinder engine into a motor cycle frame were two-fold. Set the engine across the frame, and in addition to its width there would be difficulties in arranging a primary drive; put it in line with the frame, and the wheelbase becomes unwieldy (and, besides, there was often overheating of the third cylinder from the front). But Edward Turner had thought up a novel solution to both the width and wheelbase problems, and his cigarette-packet sketch showed the four cylinders arranged two-by-two, in effect two vertical twins mounted one behind the other.

During the First World War, Edward had lied about his age, joining the Merchant Navy as a radio operator when he was scarcely 16 years old, but peacetime found him dealing in ex-military motor cycles and, eventually, opening a motor cycle business in Dulwich, South London. But buying and selling did not interest him greatly, and his main ambition was to get into motor cycle manufacture. He did, too, in a small way, building a sporty-looking 350 cc single with a chain-driven overhead camshaft in the back room of his Dulwich premises.

Whether or not the Turner Special was ever marketed is debatable, but at least it achieved some sort of fame by being listed, together with a photograph, in the 1927 edition of *The Motor Cycle*'s annual Buyer's Guide. Furthermore, the listing of the Turner Special meant that Edward was not entirely an unknown when, in late 1928, he brought his Great Idea to the Midlands. Selling the scheme, though, was something else, and one after another the major factories turned him down. AJS showed some interest, but nothing came of it. Finally, he sought an interview with Jack Sangster,

who ran the Ariel works at Selly Oak, Birmingham.

'I want to see the finished drawings before making a decision,' said Jack, 'but I'll back you to the extent of providing you with an office where you can get on with it.' In fact he did better than that, because he gave Edward the exclusive services of a junior draughtsman – a lad named Bert Hopwood, who had joined Ariel on leaving school, and whose first job had been tea-boy in the Ariel foundry – to expedite the work.

There were to be eighteen months of intensive development, and construction of a series of mock-ups and experimental prototypes before the first production-model Ariel Square Four could be revealed in all its glory. The first prototype of all was so light and compact that it made use of a standard Ariel 250 cc frame; in addition, it was a unit-construction job, with a three-speed gearbox gear-driven from the rear of the two parallel crankshafts.

To convince sceptics that the 'ten mph to a hundred in top' slogan was not advertising eyewash, Freddie Clarke took a 1,000 cc pushrod Ariel Square Four to Brooklands in 1936 – and did exactly what the slogan said. Behind the bike, standing, are designer Edward Turner (*left*) and service manager, Ernie Smith

Following pages: perhaps the most significant new British bike of the late 1930s was Edward Turner's 500 cc Triumph Speed Twin. The original 1937 model with six-stud cylinder base flange was replaced for the following season by an eight-stud version

Works trials rider Harry Perrey (who died in 1978) was involved, also, in experimental testing at Selly Oak. 'It was a delightful little thing,' he told the author, a few years ago. 'Drop it into gear, sit side-saddle and you could push-start it with one shove of the foot. Perhaps if Ariels had stuck to that initial conception they could still have been making Square Fours today.'

Well, perhaps, but the shrewd Jack Sangster had his own reasons for insisting on a modification of the design. Unit-construction was out, for a start, because Ariels were committed to using Burman gearboxes; and for economic reasons the Square Four had to employ the same frame, with widely-splayed front down tubes, as that of a Val Page-designed 500 cc sloper single.

It was hardly surprising that visitors to the 1930 Olympia Show in London gaped in wonder, because the newly-announced 500 cc Ariel Square Four was almost as compact as a single. It had a single overhead camshaft, driven by chain, and the two crankshafts were coupled by helical gears in the middle of each shaft. Three of the crank throws were overhung. The exception was the left-hand rear, where the shaft was extended to carry the chain drive to a conventional four-speed Burman gearbox.

The crankcase was split horizontally, and when the sump was dropped it could be seen that the two crankshafts were carried in trunnion bearings suspended from the crankcase upper section. A half-speed shaft was driven by gearing from the forward crankshaft, and on its right-hand end were two chain drives. One of these led to a special four-spark Magdyno ignition and lighting unit, while the other, tensioned by a spring-loaded Weller blade (possibly the first use of this device in motor cycle design) drove the camshaft.

Turner's intention was for the Square Four to be an ultra-smooth light tourer, but sidecar enthusiasts saw it as the ideal family slogger – except that it needed more power than was currently on offer. So the Ariel company duly obliged by introducing a 600 cc version for 1932, and that one was so popular that it pushed the 500 cc model out of the pro-gramme.

Nevertheless, the six-hundred was not all that it might have been. It was rather short on flywheel effect – and with an overhung-crank layout, that was something the factory could not rectify easily. Another drawback was that the cylinder head was insufficiently finned, and with an inadequate air flow across the head the engine suffered from overheat-ing. It was this factor which had caused Ben Bickell so many headaches, in his unsuccessful quest for The

Motor Cycle's 'hundred in the hour' cup.

By November, 1935, a complete redesign had been undertaken, and the new Square Four was a 997 cc machine affording '10 to 100 in top gear'. The four cylinders were still arranged two-by-two, but almost everything else had changed. Now there were full (not overhung) cranks throughout, and the two crankshafts were connected by gears in a separate chamber at the right-hand side of the crankcase assembly. The overhead camshafts had gone, and valve operation was by pushrods. For a further season the 600 cc model continued as before but eventually that, too, was exchanged for a pushrod ohv version.

By that time, however, Edward Turner had taken on new responsibilities. Up to 1936 the Triumph plant at Coventry built cars, motor cycles and pedal cycles, but the management felt that diversification of that kind was no longer practical. Their future, they felt, lay in car manufacture; and so they sold off the bicycle manufacturing rights, and were prepar-ing to drop motor cycle manufacture entirely.

However, Ariel boss Jack Sangster got to hear of the plan and, in the course of a train journey between Coventry and London, hammered out a scheme for survival of the name with the representative of Triumph's bankers. By the time the train steamed into London, the Triumph name was his, together with an option on part of the Triumph works, and on the motor cycle manufacturing machinery it contained.

To the surprise of many people, the man he appointed to run the Triumph firm – not only as designer, but as managing director – was Edward Turner. Agreed, Turner was a good designer, the Square Four proved that much; but as an adminis-trator he was an unknown quantity.

Yet Sangster had picked wisely. Turner, often morose and difficult to work with, had the knack of never spending tuppence where three-ha'pence would do, and his economies soon stemmed the losses the motor cycle side of Triumph had been enduring. More than that, he was an instinctive stylist, and the cosmetic touches he applied to the Val Page range of Triumph Mk.V singles – as the 250 cc Tiger 70, 350 cc Tiger 80 and 500 cc Tiger 90, they were given a more rounded fuel tank shape, fashionable upswept exhaust pipes, and a finish of silver outlined in blue, with plenty of chromium plating – had the customers queuing up at dealers' doors.

Top of the pre-Sangster Triumph range had been a majestic 650 cc vertical twin from the drawing-board of Val Page, but that model was dropped by

The Ariel Square Four, as first manufactured, employed an overhead camshaft. This is the 1932 600 cc ohc model, new features of which embraced a redesigned cylinder head, and an instrument panel inset in the tank top face

the incoming management and, instead, Turner designed a vertical twin of his own (he could, at times, be jealous of other people's work). Announced in July, 1937 as the Model T, it soon adopted the name Speed Twin and the catalogue listing of 5T.

Making use of his dictum that every part of an engine had to be as light as possible commensurate with the work it had to do, he evolved an engine only 5 lb heavier than the 500 cc Tiger 90 single – and sitting so comfortably in the Tiger 90 frame that it could almost have been designed for it.

A bolted-up crankshaft was specified, with the two cranks bolted through flanges to a massive central flywheel. Pistons rose and fell together, on connecting rods forged in RR56 light alloy. The inlet camshaft was set across the rear of the engine, the

exhaust camshaft was across the front, and the pushrods were contained in chromium-plated tubes. Reputed power output was 26 bhp at 6,000 rpm – not good by today's standards, but pretty impressive for 1937, and quite enough to give the Speed Twin a 90 mph potential.

The machine was an instant success – mainly because the fickle public, while clamouring for the smoothness of a twin, wanted also something that looked like the singles with which they had been so familiar for years; and that was just where the Speed Twin scored. It *did* look like a conventional two-port single, while under way its exhaust was a gentle purr, not a bark.

Turner's follow-up, for the 1939 season, was a more sporting version of the Speed Twin to which he gave the name of Tiger 100 – the figure giving an indication of its speed potential. Primarily the Tiger 100 was a super-sports roadster, but it could be used also for clubman racing, to which end it was

119

From Selly Oak, Birmingham, came what many an enthusiast will claim was the ultimate in classic British singles, the Ariel Red Hunter. Seen here is a 497 cc Model VH of January, 1937, basically a Val Page design to which was given the magic touch of master cosmetician Edward Turner

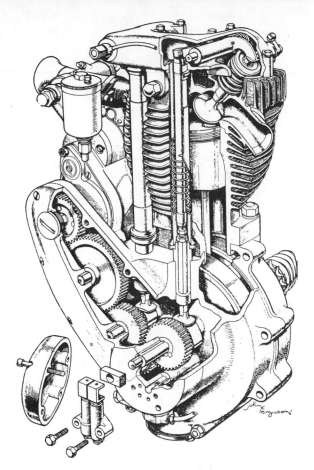

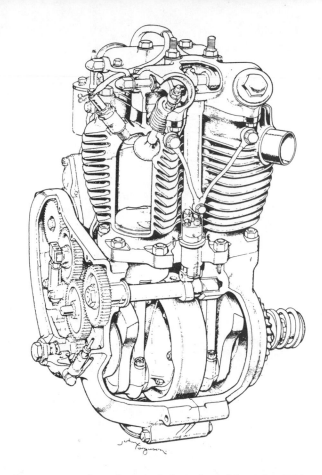

equipped with a very ingenious form of silencer of conical shape. Remove the detachable cap, tail pipe and baffles, and the machine stood revealed as a racer, complete with track megaphones.

The speed boys had taken to the Triumph Twin even before the Tiger 100 version was launched, Ernie Lyons (who was to win the 1946 Manx Grand Prix in driving rain on a Triumph) using one for Irish racing; Lyons, too, rode it in the 1938 Manx Grand Prix with unfortunate results, because he crashed into a marshal's telephone hut on the exit from Ramsey, and put the whole telephone circuit for the mountain section of the course out of action until repairs could be effected.

At Brooklands, Ivan Wicksteed drove a supercharged Speed Twin to an all-time 500 cc lap record of 118·02 mph. Triumph development engineer Freddie Clarke bored-out a Speed Twin to 501 cc (so that he would not be competing against the firm's own customers) and raced that, breaking the 750 cc Outer Circuit record at 118·6 mph – and, for good measure, setting an all-time 350 cc Brooklands lap record of 105·97 mph, with a Tiger 80.

It is said that Turner drew the inspiration for the Triumph Twin from an experiment carried out at the Ariel works with one of the early prototype Square Fours, when the front crankshaft was removed, to allow the engine to function as a vertical twin. Watching the experiment, also, were Val Page and Bert Hopwood, both of whom would later design vertical twins of their own. Certainly the Speed Twin was to be the springboard for many other twins of similar layout in the years ahead and, had the 1939 London Show taken place, at least four more from other manufacturers would have made their debut.

There would also have been a 350 cc twin from Edward Turner's own drawing-board. This was due for announcement the week that war was declared, and some copies of *The Motor Cycle* had already been printed with the banner line 'New British 350 cc Twin' on the cover when an urgent call from Coventry brought the presses to a halt. Another and much duller headline ('Modern Fork Design Analysed') was substituted and the presses began again – and it would be six long and weary years before the new machine, the Model 3T, reached the market.

Consolidation and apprehension

The middle years of the 1930s can now be considered in a wider field. If British road-users had the feeling that they were being 'got at', they had good reason. Leslie Hore-Belisha was now the Minister of Transport, an energetic character who was to leave his name to posterity as the originator of the pedestrian crossings that began to pepper the city streets, each crossing place being marked by orange-topped black-and-white poles which rapidly became known as Belisha Beacons.

For the first time, an official booklet of recommended road behaviour (termed the Highway Code) was drawn up, and distributed free to each household. Various new petty restrictions included a ban on sounding the horn of a stationary vehicle between the hours of 11.30 pm and 7 am.

But registration of new motor cycles was still rising, especially in the 250 cc class, and by early 1935 one bike in every three sold was a two-fifty. Less happily, three-wheeler sales were starting to slip, mainly because they had not been given equivalent tax concessions in the Easter Budget, but the three-wheeler fancier still had a remarkably wide choice. Not only was there the inevitable Morgan (with the vee-twin models augmented by a more sophisticated three-wheeler powered by a Ford car engine), but BSA had added a four-cylinder water-cooled job to their air-cooled vee-twin, Coventry Victor offered flat-twins of 850 or 998 cc, and Raleigh's unusual single-front-wheel Safety Seven – new at the 1933 Show – was attracting many buyers.

Produced in a one-time shirt factory in Ringwood, Hants, the little 500 cc JMB (the initials were those of George H. Jones, Ray Mason, and Cecil Barrow) had begun life as a simple little single-cylinder three-wheeler at a realistic price, and in its first year it sold well enough to give its sponsors a tiny profit. But JMB dealers felt that the model would be improved if certain changes were made and so, obligingly, for 1935 the JMB had become a glossier and more fully-equipped job at, naturally, a correspondingly higher cost. Yet whatever the dealers may have imagined, the public did not want to know and so the JMB disappeared, a victim of unwanted elaboration.

By 1935, the sporting side of motor cycling had expanded considerably, and the enthusiast, that Easter, was offered a very wide choice of meetings. There were sand races, short circuit events, grass tracks, scrambles, sprints and hill-climbs (the last including the famous Red Marley, near Stourport, where the BBC were broadcasting a live commentary on the efforts of Bert Perrigo and company to surmount the 1-in-2 slope). The sprint venues included Gatwick Racecourse, where on the concrete strip in front of the grandstand Eric Fernihough took a British bike into the 'elevens' for the first time, by clocking a standing-quarter-mile time of 11·72 sec with his blown 996 cc Brough Superior. On the blown Ariel Square Four with which he had failed to get the 'hundred in the hour' cup, Ben Bickell took second fastest time of the day with 12·49 sec.

Faster still, though, was Ernst Henne, who wheeled out the works-prepared 750 cc BMW and, on the Frankfurt Autobahn in Germany, set a new 'world's fastest' record of 159·1 mph.

Raleigh adopted a rather unusual approach, in evolving their first passenger three-wheeler. Introduced late in 1932, it employed the 5 cwt Raleigh commercial van chassis. The vehicle was unsuccessful, and was soon withdrawn, to be replaced eventually by the Safety Seven

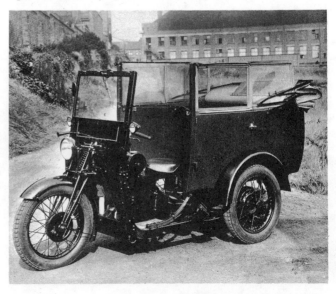

123

Above: a look at German design in the late 1930s. This 1938 Victoria 250 cc Aero two-stroke featured an oilbath rear chaincase, and a frame formed in part from two pressings seam-welded together. In 1966, Victoria amalgamated with DKW and Hercules to form Zweirad-Union

Below: classic sports-roadster of its period was the 350 cc overhead-camshaft Velocette Model KSS, derived from the same firm's racing machines. In Mk. II form it was built from 1936 to 1948, employing the light-alloy cylinder head seen on this 1938 example

Although the Rudge is considered as one of the classic British machines of the 1930s, the truth is that the makers were in financial trouble for years, and were finally rescued by the His Master's Voice record company. This 1938 495 cc four-valve Special was one of the last to be built in Coventry before production moved down to Hayes

Perhaps the most illustrious Brough Superior fan of all time was Col T. E. Lawrence ('Lawrence of Arabia'). He is seen collecting a new model, his sixth, from the Brough Superior works at Nottingham in 1933. George Brough, with walking sticks, was recovering from a crash in the ISDT

Nearer home, the petrol pumps that for years had dispensed the familiar Pratt's fuel gained new oval globes, lettered 'Esso'. Plans were announced for a projected new road tunnel under the River Thames from Dartford to Purfleet; but it was to be many years before those plans became a reality.

Stark tragedy struck when national hero Colonel Lawrence of Arabia, a Brough Superior enthusiast of many years' standing, swerved to avoid the erratically-ridden bicycle of a butcher's errand boy, struck the kerb and was killed. Another motor cycle accident, this time near Meriden, took the life of Norton's brilliant Arthur Carrol, the young designer whose work would live for many years in the overhead-camshaft engine known the world over as the Manx Norton.

As the autumn days of 1935 shortened, so the motor cycle press began to carry news of the next season's models. Velocette, for example, were entering the 500 cc market for the first time since pre-First World War days, with the short-pushrod MSS roadster, a development of the 250 cc MOV and 350 cc MAC models of the same layout. The Ariel

Square Four had been completely redesigned, and now emerged as a pushrod ohv machine of 1,000 cc (although the 600 cc ohc job remained available), the two crankshafts of which were coupled by gearing on the left, not in the centre.

The Olympia Show brought still more novelties, one of the more significant of which was a humble little 125 cc Villiers power unit. And 'unit' was the operative word, because Villiers had broken with tradition by building a neat little power egg with integral three-speed gearbox. It had, too, a light-alloy cylinder head, and a flat-top piston. In the years to come there would be unit-construction Villiers packages of various capacities, but the little 125 cc was first of the line, and although the only manufacturer to exhibit a complete bike making use of it was Wolf, other firms were already building prototypes.

Most eye-catching model at Olympia was the massive 500 cc AJS overhead-camshaft vee-four, shown in air-cooled roadster form 'with provision for supercharger'. As so happens, the four never did go into commercial production, but it was to form the basis of an exotic racer which, with the addition of water-cooling and a blower, very nearly had its day in the Ulster Grand Prix.

Since 1932 BSA had been manufacturing a very pretty overhead-valve 500 cc vee-twin (the Model J12), originally to Army contract but later for police duties and, eventually, for the civilian market also. Now, that machine was joined by a 750 cc twin on similar lines. OK Supreme offered a model with a 350 cc overhead-camshaft engine of their own design. Brough Superior featured hairpin valve springs on their magnificent 1,000 cc SS100 ohv twin. Rudge announced a competitions version of the much-admired four-valve Ulster, for trials or scrambles use and derived from the machine with which Bob McGregor had won that year's Scottish Six Days Trial.

Highlight of the Triumph stand was a catalogued racer, the Model 5/10, heading a lengthy Val Page range of ohv and sv singles plus, of course, the Page-designed Model 6/1 650 cc vertical twin. Unknown to the Show-going public, however, Colonel Sir Claude V. Holbrook (in overall control of the Triumph firm) had already taken the decision to discontinue Triumph motor cycle manufacture on 31 December, 1935.

His reasons seemed logical enough. Triumph had occupied a multi-storey and rather inefficient works in Priory Street, Coventry (now covered partly by the city's modern swimming pool, partly by the De Vere hotel, and partly by Coventry Cathedral), but

Quite evidently, Mr F. Hayes, of Holland Park, London, did not suffer from claustrophobia! This two-wheeled car was built around a 500 cc AJS in 1936, and its constructor used it to tour extensively

car production was being moved out to more suitable premises. This would have left the Priory Street works under-occupied, and worthy though the existing motor cycle range undoubtedly was, it was by no means selling in sufficient numbers to warrant retaining the old works.

But as explained in the previous section, Jack Sangster staged a rescue in the nick of time. Under his regime, Triumph motor cycle production was concentrated into the Dale Street end of the old works, and the vacated part of the property was due to be taken over by the city council for redevelopment; except that Hitler got there first and, in the Coventry blitz of 1941, the German bombers flattened the lot, the occupied as well as the unoccupied parts of the factory.

By this time, the growing military strength of Germany and the ever-more-ominous posturing of Adolf Hitler could no longer be ignored. BSA management, as early as 1935, had sensed the coming troubles ahead and, on their own initiative, brought gun-making equipment out of mothballs, to re-equip part of the Small Heath plant for armament production; an order for 16,000 rifles for the Iraq Government served to run-in machinery idle since 1918.

Gradually, the British re-armament programme got under way, in so doing putting extra spending money into the pockets of the workers. Motor cycle sales boomed to such a degree that by 1937 one vehicle in every five on British roads was a two-wheeler. It was the re-armament programme, too, (or, more accurately, the hope of sharing that programme) which helped Douglas out of one of its frequent financial holes.

The British Aircraft Company, of London Air Park, Feltham (now part of Heathrow) formed a new concern known as Aero Engines Ltd and, in anticipation of receiving a contract to build Hispano-Suiza aircraft engines under licence, took over the Douglas motor cycle works at Bristol. But the contract did not come, and while the Bristol plant ticked over, motor cycle production continued on a reduced scale, for sale through one outlet only, that of London dealers Pride and Clarke Ltd.

Denmark's national motor cycle, the four-in-line 746 cc Nimbus was in production from 1920 to 1955. This 1938 model, with channel-steel frame, shaft drive, and telescopic front fork, is entirely typical of a design that changed but little over the years. The makers, Fisker and Nielsen, are better-known nowadays as manufacturers of Nilfisk vacuum cleaners and washing machines

The 350 cc side-valve BSA Model B23 de Luxe had a life of one season only. Introduced for 1939, it was superseded for 1940 by a lighter model based on the C11 two-fifty. This particular example was first supplied by Cope's of Birmingham

Top: the 'upside-down' Indian Four of 1936. Originally, the four-in-line Indian had been an Ace design, but for 1936 the engine was completely redesigned by Briggs Weaver, and instead of an inlet-over-exhaust valve arrangement became exhaust-over-inlet. Engine capacity was a colossal 1,206 cc

Above: first built for Army use, the 500 cc ohv BSA J12 was later adopted for police work. Some also reached the civilian market; this 1936 example has a forged steel backbone frame

Payment for re-armament was another matter, and road users were incensed when, in April, 1936, Neville Chamberlain announced that he saw no reason why the Road Fund (the revenue from car and motor cycle taxation which, supposedly, was to be devoted to road construction and repair) should not be treated as general revenue, and he would, therefore, be directing almost £6 million of motor taxation receipts into the exchequer.

The Army, meanwhile, was considering replacement of its motor cycles. It had had a batch of vee-twin BSAs, supplied to WD specification in 1932, but the majority of service machines were still elderly side-valves, such as the 550 cc NSD Triumph, and

350 cc 1929 Douglas. Rudge, BSA and Norton were invited to submit more up-to-date machines for 10,000-mile evaluation trials. Norton's contribution was the Model 16H, and it was this model which won the day.

An urgent contract for 100 military models was passed to Nortons, because a state of emergency had arisen in Palestine, and a contingent of British troops was being sent out to police the country. Also, the factory was advised to make ready for a much bigger contract, which could be on its way if the situation in Europe became more serious than it was already.

By comparison with Germany's factory and government-backed attempts at holding on to the prestigious 'world's fastest' title, Britain had to pin her hopes on one man operating on little more than a shoestring. That man was Eric Fernihough, who took his 996 cc Brough Superior to Gyon, in Hungary, and there annexed the flying mile record at 163·82 mph – collecting the pitiful bonus of just £25. Alas, too, it was not the 'world's fastest', Ernst Henne having pushed the flying kilometre speed up to 169 mph only a few days before.

The title battle raged into 1937, now with Piero Taruffi joining in, using the four-cylinder Gilera dressed in peculiarly tall streamlining. In his first session he took twelve assorted records including the five-mile and ten-mile at speeds up to 154·933 mph. Fernihough and the Brough pushed the 'flying kilo' to 170 mph, and Taruffi clocked 170·373 mph – only to have his figure rejected as a record because he had not bettered Ferni's time by the required half-second.

Later in the same week Henne returned to the fray, with a new flying-fish streamlined BMW built by Rudolph Schleicher and featuring air-brake fins on the tail. The new bike was unsteady, however, and was sent back to the BMW factory for further wind-tunnel testing.

Again Eric Fernihough took his Brough to Hungary, with his 'scalded cat' symbol painted on the head fairing. Sadly, a gust of wind caught the bike when Eric was at full speed. He veered off the straight but narrow road and crashed with fatal results.

At the end of 1937, Nortons could still claim that they had won more road races than any other make (Velocette, too, had done pretty well in the 350 cc class), but the 1938 racing story would be a rather less happy one so far as Bracebridge Street was concerned.

BMW, in particular, were out for glory and their teamsters, Karl Gall and Georg Meier, had already

Top: most consistent world speed record holder of the 1930s was Ernst Henne, who between 1929 and 1937 collected a total of 76 records. He is seen in November, 1937, after his 500 cc BMW had pushed the world's fastest figure to 173·675 mph on the Frankfurt Autobahn

Above: Eric Fernihough parades his 'Scalded Cat' semi-streamlined Brough Superior world record challenger before the Crystal Palace crowds. It was on this machine that he met his death in 1938 at Gyon, in Hungary, during a 180 mph run

Opposite, top: certainly the most complicated racer of British origin was the vee-four AJS. In its final, water-cooled and supercharged form, it is seen on Portstewart seafront in the hands of Bob Foster, during the 1939 North West 200. The machine is now owned by Sammy Miller

reached the Isle of Man in April, 1938, for an intensive course of circuit-learning with Jock West as headmaster. Still air-cooled at this stage, the

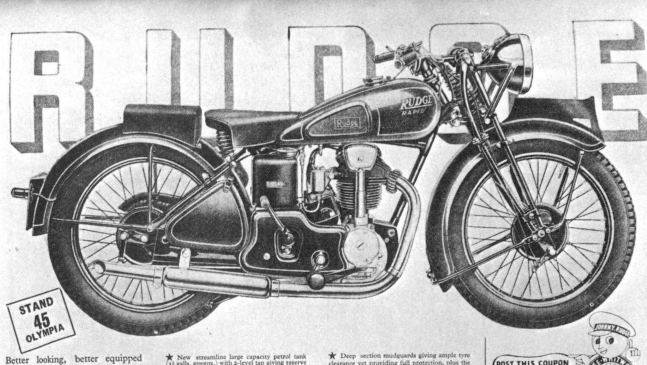

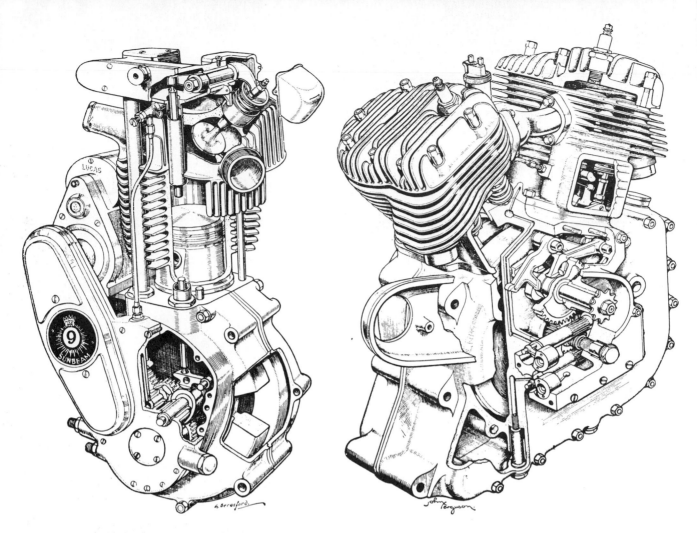

Above: a classic from the original John Marston stable was the 493 cc Sunbeam Model 9. The final Wolverhampton development, seen here, embraced an internal oil pump and enclosed overhead valve gear. The year was 1937

Above, right: new for 1937 was this imposing 1,140 cc vee-twin side-valve by Royal Enfield, with oil carried in a crankcase extension, and no fewer than four reciprocating-plunger oil pumps. A slogger, the big Enfield was intended principally for commercial sidecar haulage

complicated AJS four had adopted a Zoller blower operating at 6 lb boost, and George Rowley was testing it on the short manufacturers' circuit at Donington Park. There would be a rotary-valve DKW for the Lightweight (250 cc) TT, but Moto Guzzi would not be in the Isle of Man this time – because, they said, the TT Races clashed with a summit meeting between Adolf Hitler and Benito Mussolini (although it is difficult to understand what *that* had to do with it!).

Probably the most novel power unit ever to be seen in the Isle of Man was this flat-twin two-stroke, which was designed, built, and entered by Colin Taylor. Both pistons operated in the same cylinder and flew outward, where rocking beams transferred motion to the longitudinal crankshaft; other oddities embraced an all-chain gearbox and rotary inlet valve

Nortons themselves had made a few modifications to the works models. Notably, there was full springing employing an undamped telescopic front fork and plunger-type rear suspension. The engine had a shorter stroke, and a finned crankcase into which the cylinder barrel was much more deeply sunk than before. And conical wheel hubs were making their first appearance.

Two of the blown vee-four AJS models, ridden by

Top: an unusual machine with which to contest the 1939 Senior TT was this 346 cc DKW, not a works model but privately owned and ridden by Fergus Anderson. He finished 26th after an undistinguished ride

Above: works Nortons were equipped with telescopic forks and plunger rear springing in 1938. In that year's Senior TT, Freddie Frith crosses the line in third place, victory having gone to team-mate Harold Daniell

Rowley and Bob Foster, were given a try-out in the Leinster 200, although without success, but it was a more promising debut for the latest 350 cc Velocette, with Stanley Woods in the saddle.

Practice for the 1938 TT Races brought out a machine which, incredibly, was even noisier than the DKW (of which it had been said that its descent of Bray Hill could be heard in Blackpool). The din-machine was Colin Taylor's home-built CBT, a flat-twin two-stroke, the construction of which defies short description. Such was the racket that Colin's wife resorted to towing him, by car, to a less-inhabited area of the island when there were experiments to be carried out; but Taylor never did

For sheer, effortless performance, this 1939 1,100 cc Brough Superior side-valve twin was untouchable. The engine is a specially-built Matchless product, and the gearbox is a Sturmey-Archer-Norton

get the CBT to run satisfactorily and it failed to qualify.

Practice, too, brought problems for BMW when Gall cast himself adrift and was taken to hospital. Georg Meier stripped a plug-hole thread on the start line, and it was Harold Daniell who again gave Nortons a Senior TT victory, with a 91 mph record lap that was to stay unbroken until, in 1950, a lithe youngster named Geoff Duke happened along. But Germany did indeed get its first TT success, when Ewald Kluge brought home his DKW ahead of a whole string of Excelsior Manxman riders (so many, in fact, that every first-class replica except the winner's was won on an Excelsior; the same make also provided the club team and maker's team winners).

Winner of the Junior race was Stanley Woods, providing Velocette with their first Isle of Man victory since 1929. Incidentally, the same TT week had seen a supplementary attraction in the shape of the first Isle of Man Grand National scramble, held over a very boggy stretch of moorland adjacent to Windy Corner. First three home were Cliff Clegg (350 cc BSA), Allan Jefferies (350 cc Triumph) and Len Heath (500 cc Ariel); but the drawback from the organisers' viewpoint was that only a wire fence separated the course from the mountain road, and regrettably few spectators bothered to come in via the paying gate!

Back on the mainland, several police forces were co-operating in a 'courtesy cops' campaign, the intention being to improve road behaviour 'by example and advice' instead of by entering names in a little black book. Also, the Commissioner of Metropolitan Police was calling for 2,500 motor cycling volunteers, to become members of the Special War Reserve Police. Matchless reported that they had been given 'a substantial order' for 350 cc machines (essentially the Model G3 Clubman, with military modifications) for the British Army.

The widest choice —— and at prices to suit all pockets

Francis-Barnett

Stand 39 Olympia

MODELS & PRICES

Model	Description	Price
"Plover G/40"	148 c.c., direct lighting	£26.10.0
"Plover G/41"	148 c.c., flywheel mag., dynamo lighting	£29.10.0
"Seagull G/43"	249 c.c. long stroke, flywheel mag., dynamo lighting	£33.10.0
"Cruiser G/39"	249 c.c. long stroke, coil ignition, dynamo lighting	£38.15.0
"Cruiser G/45"	249 c.c. deflectorless piston engine, dynamo lighting	£41.0.0
"Stag G/44"	248 c.c. O.H.V., dynamo lighting	£46.0.0
"Red Stag G/46"	248 c.c. O.H.V., dynamo lighting, sports equipment	£48.0.0

Shows *clean* motorcycling at economical cost

"Cruiser G/45"

FRANCIS & BARNETT LTD., COVENTRY.

Fall of the curtain

That Europe was fast moving towards a state of war was becoming all too clear – the digging of air-raid slit-trenches in London's Hyde Park was only one manifestation – and the proposed introduction of a six-month period of National Service for the under-20s of Britain was accepted philosophically. From everywhere there were calls for motor cyclists to be ready in case of emergency, to serve with the war reserve police (George Formby's film comedy, *Spare a Copper* dealt with this aspect), the auxiliary fire service, and the Territorial Army.

This was the period of the 1938 'Munich Crisis', and although the British Prime Minister flew back from his summit meeting with Hitler, to display a paper which, he said, guaranteed 'Peace in our time', the country was taking no chances. Nortons announced that they would not be fielding a racing team for the 1939 season, because of the pressure of work on military contracts; the factory duplicated its jigs and tooling for the 16H side-valve, but even that would not be enough to meet demand, and the Army authorities now brought BSA into the action. Indeed, the Small Heath works were to provide 3,000 500 cc M20 side-valves in the run-up to September, 1939, but in addition a military version of the 350 cc ohv B29 was submitted for evaluation. This was accepted, and an order for 10,000 B29s was sent to BSA, but only 200 were made before the contract was changed to the M20, for the sake of consistency.

The 1938 Earls Court Show brought a sensational new Brough Superior, the shaft-drive, flat-four Dream, in which both Ike Hatch and Freddie Dixon had had a hand. An AJS highlight was the ohc Model 7R racer (yes, they *did* use the designation in pre-war days). Now under AMC control, Sunbeam showed a high-camshaft design (by Bert Collier) with a vast timing case on which the Sunbeam name was scrawled. Douglas were back – but, ominously, the New Imperial stand was darkened and unmanned, while a bailiff sat bowler-hatted among the hopefully-intended 1939 New Imps.

A corner of Sotwell, Berkshire

What a line-up of road-racing talent! Left to right, they are Jock West, Dave Whitworth, Ernie Thomas, Freddie Frith, and Ted Mellors – and all, according to the publicity agent, had tried out and approved the 80 cc Levis-engined HEC autocycle in the foreground, at the 1938 London Show

Explanation of the latter situation was that Norman Downs, founder and long-serving boss of New Imperial had died, and although orders for the machines remained at a high level, farmed-out work had proved costly to rectify. Still, the name would not die yet, because Jack Sangster – already the saviour of Ariel and Triumph – now came to an arrangement with the liquidator (Mr Graham, oddly enough the same Midland Bank nominee with whom Jack had dealt when acquiring Triumph). New Imperial creditors would be paid off in full, and production was to continue at the Spring Road, Hall Green works until the first week of September, 1939, after which production would transfer to vacant space in Triumph's Coventry plant.

On the road-racing front, the challenge from Italy and Germany was overwhelming. In the Grand Prix of Europe, winner Georg Meier proved that the BMW was now not only quick but had overcome earlier handling problems, by beating the lap record six times. Trying desperately hard, Harold Daniell wiped off one of the Norton's footrests against the kerb (it flew into the crowd, and cut a woman spectator's arm) but held on to second place, with Freddie Frith third on another Norton. In the 350 cc class, Crasher White (Norton) managed to hold off a pair of very fast DKWs – but there was paddock gossip that DKW were developing four-piston twins, while NSU had a new 350 cc overhead-camshaft vertical twin.

The North-West 200 race, in Northern Ireland, produced a surprise result when Bob Foster, on the blown AJS four lost time at the start and Stanley Woods dropped out with a seized engine; instead, the chequered flag went out for Ernie Lyons, on a

The Royal Enfield 125 cc 'Flying Flea' originated as a frank copy of the 98 cc DKW, even to the style of painting, at the request of DKW's erstwhile Dutch agents. During the Second World War, it was to earn praise as a parachute-drop lightweight, and for shepherding troops on the Normandy beach-heads

Triumph Speed Twin!

The Manx Grand Prix remained obstinately British, and there was but one foreign machine in the entire 1938 entry. Oddly enough, it was a DKW ridden by Sheffield speedway ace Frank Varey, but although 'El Diabolo Rojo' was lying fourth at one stage in the Lightweight event he then came off, and it was Denis Parkinson (Excelsior) who won the class.

Britain could also still claim a 100 per cent record of 350 cc wins in international road-racing, with Ted Mellors (Velocette) as European Champion. We had won the International Six Days Trial for the third year in succession. And there was news that Velocette were at work on a potential world-beater, a supercharged vertical twin with shaft drive.

In other fields, both Britain and France now had over half a million motor cyclists on the road, although that figure was far surpassed by Germany's total of 1,327,000. Italy's figure was not revealed, but that country was due to remove all taxation from motor cycles by February, 1939, and there were plans afoot for the production of a national 200 cc machine – a kind of Volksbike – to be sold to the populace through a savings scheme.

British Army participation in trials was growing mightily, and there were no fewer than 29 Army entries in the snowy 1939 Colmore Cup Trial. But the big sensation came with the Victory Trial, where the team award went to the trio from the 2nd Battallion, Royal Tank Corps, comprising Corporals Paddy Doyle and Fred Rist, and Private Jackie Wood.

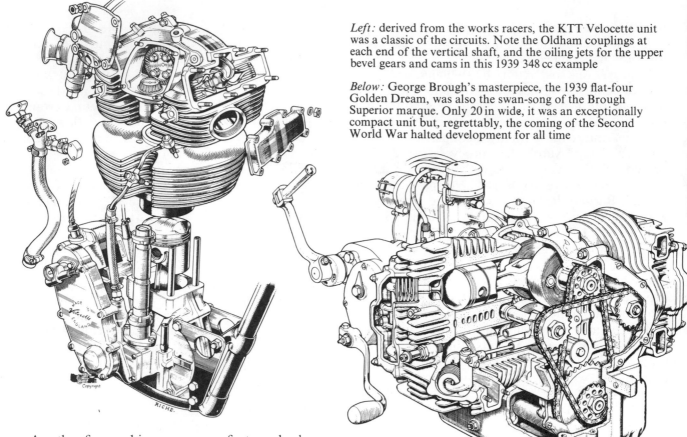

Left: derived from the works racers, the KTT Velocette unit was a classic of the circuits. Note the Oldham couplings at each end of the vertical shaft, and the oiling jets for the upper bevel gears and cams in this 1939 348 cc example

Below: George Brough's masterpiece, the 1939 flat-four Golden Dream, was also the swan-song of the Brough Superior marque. Only 20 in wide, it was an exceptionally compact unit but, regrettably, the coming of the Second World War halted development for all time

Another former big-name manufacturer had gone under. This time it was Calthorpe, but the name was bought by Bruce Douglas, of the Bristol bike-building family, and it was Bruce's intention to continue the make (but using AJS engines) with premises at Bristol Airport. Unfortunately, the project failed to get beyond the prototype stage before war brought a close-down.

Abroad, the Dutch distributors for DKW (Stokvis and Sonen) ran into race discrimination when DKW discovered that Stokvis had Jewish directors and, under Hitler's anti-Semetic ruling, cut off supplies. Undaunted, Stokvis then approached the Royal Enfield company, and the upshot was a small two-stroke identical with the 98 cc DKW (Holland's best-seller) right down to the rubber-band suspension of the front fork, and the silver-wing style of tank side panel; the only difference was that the Royal Enfield version (the Model RE) employed a deflector-top instead of flat-top piston, and capacity had risen to 125 cc.

Ironically, the little RE (irreverently termed the Flying Flea) would later serve with the Airborne Forces, while on the opposing side the Wehrmacht used the 98 cc DKW for behind-the-lines duty.

A news item from February, 1939 pointed a new trend in home entertainment, because Britain was operating the world's first regular television service –

and TV addicts were pressing for the compulsory suppression of vehicle ignition systems. It is intriguing to note, too, that the 1939 BBC programmes included a documentary showing motor cycle-mounted 'courtesy cops' at work.

Over the years, many factories had made attempts to win the Maudes' Trophy, awarded by the ACU for what it considered the most meritorious demonstration of a machine's capabilities in any given year, and 1939 found no fewer than three makers determined to have a go. All 'Maudes' attempts had to be carried out under ACU observation, and in the full glare of publicity, so there could be no sweeping it under the carpet, should any stunt fail to come off.

Triumph were the first to try, in March, 1939, with an extended test of a Speed Twin and a Tiger 100 which took in speed tests at Donington Park, Brooklands, and an impressive road mileage. Next to try were BSA, with a round-England trip and 25 climbs of Bwlch-y-Groes in the dark. Then it was Panther's turn to blast a big single (the 600 cc Model 100) up and down the Great North Road from Leeds to High Barnet day and night, to cover 10,000 miles in ten days. All three tests were successful, and the

merits of each were to be judged; but the results would not be known until the end of the year, and a lot could happen before then.

Registrations rose again, the 1939 figure standing 32 per cent above that of 1938, but significantly many of the new machines were 98 cc autocycles, used by district nurses, armament workers, ARP wardens, and so on. With just a couple of exceptions (HEC and Cyc-Auto), the autocycles were single-geared Villiers two-strokes, with frames by Excelsior, James, Coventry-Eagle, Norman, Dayton, Francis-Barnett, Raynal – even Rudge, the very last new model ever to bear that famous name.

June, and TT-time again, but with Norton out of the running (although the former team were allowed to use the 1938 works machinery, as private entries), a foreign victory in the Senior event was only to be expected. It came, with Georg Meier bringing the blown BMW home first, and Jock West on a second BMW taking runner-up spot. There was some consolation in Stanley Woods' Junior TT victory, on a Velocette, but Ted Mellors introduced a new element by winning the Lightweight class on a Benelli. The 'Roarer', the promised blown Velocette twin, did indeed appear during TT practice, but it was quite evidently not yet race-ready. Sadly, Harold Willis, who had nursed the 'Roarer' through its early development stages, died suddenly during TT week, a victim of meningitis; Harold, a much-loved character, had produced the world's first positive-stop foot gear change, back in 1927.

Abroad, Meier's win in the Belgian Grand Prix included a lap record at 100·63 mph, the first time the ton had been broken in a classic race, but Belgium was destined to hold the title of the World's Fastest Road Race for only a month.

It was August now, the last month of world peace, and although the BMWs were absent from the Ulster Grand Prix, Dorino Serafini was there, with the extremely potent supercharged, water-cooled, four-cylinder Gilera. Main opposition was to come from the blown, water-cooled AJS vee-fours of Bob Foster and Walter Rusk, and it was Rusk who showed that the exotic continental machinery could be challenged. The race was one to go down into history, with Rusk and Serafini locked in a bitter tussle, and Rusk breaking the lap record at over 100 mph.

Then came disaster for the AJS camp, when one of the side links of the AJS four's front forks broke, the handling went haywire, and Rusk was forced to drop out. Indeed, the Ajay was a handful at the best of times, and the factory had produced specially tough fork side links for the beast. Somehow,

though, somebody had replaced one of the special links with one from a standard touring bike – and it was that link that failed.

At the Swedish GP the BMW at last got its come-uppance, with two Gilera fours finishing ahead of Wiggerl Kraus (BMW) in the 500 cc event. Certainly Georg Meier had tried hard enough, with an over-100 mph lap record to his credit, but then Georg had cast himself off – not once, but twice. Final ignominy for Germany came in their own German Grand Prix, where full ceremonial had been arranged, in front of a grandstand-full of Nazi top brass. But it was Serafini, not Meier, who came forward to receive the trophy from a furious Korpsführer Huhnlein; and just to rub it in, Alberto Pagani, on a Moto Guzzi, beat the DKW squad to take the 250 cc honours.

In the last days of August – for that matter, the last days of peace – Bianchi announced a blown four-cylinder racer capable of producing 80 bhp at 7,500 rpm, for the 1940 season. And Donington Park ran its International Trophy meeting, which gave double victory to Freddie Frith; but the impending crisis kept the crowds away, and a number of riders, including Norton teamster Johnny Lockett, could not get to the meeting because they were on National Service.

On the morning of 3 September, 1939, the radio announced that a state of war existed between Britain and Germany. With practice due to start the next morning, and riders already in the Isle of Man, the Manx Grand Prix was cancelled. So, too, was the Earls Court Show, and although at least five new twins were known to be imminent – among them the BSA A7, Small Heath's answer to the Triumph Speed Twin, and a novel Granville Bradshaw in-line twin with ABC-type leaf rear springing from Panther, these were immediately shelved. In one sense history had repeated itself, because Panther's only other venture into the world of the twin – a vee-twin announced in 1914 – had also been killed off by the coming of war.

In the weeks that followed the declaration of war

Opposite, top, left: 1939 500 cc Matchless Super Clubman, with enclosed hairpin valve springs. From the 350 cc G3 version there evolved the wartime Matchless G3L despatch-rider model

Opposite, top, right: under AMC management, Sunbeam engine design changed radically. From the drawing board of Harry Collier, this is the high-camshaft 500 cc Sunbeam for 1939, with Weller-tensioned timing chain

Opposite, lower: Villiers entered the unit-construction market with the 125 cc three-speed engine of 1936. For 1939, this 197 cc version, known as the 'Double Century', was added. Catalogued as the Mark 5E, it was employed in the James Model K11

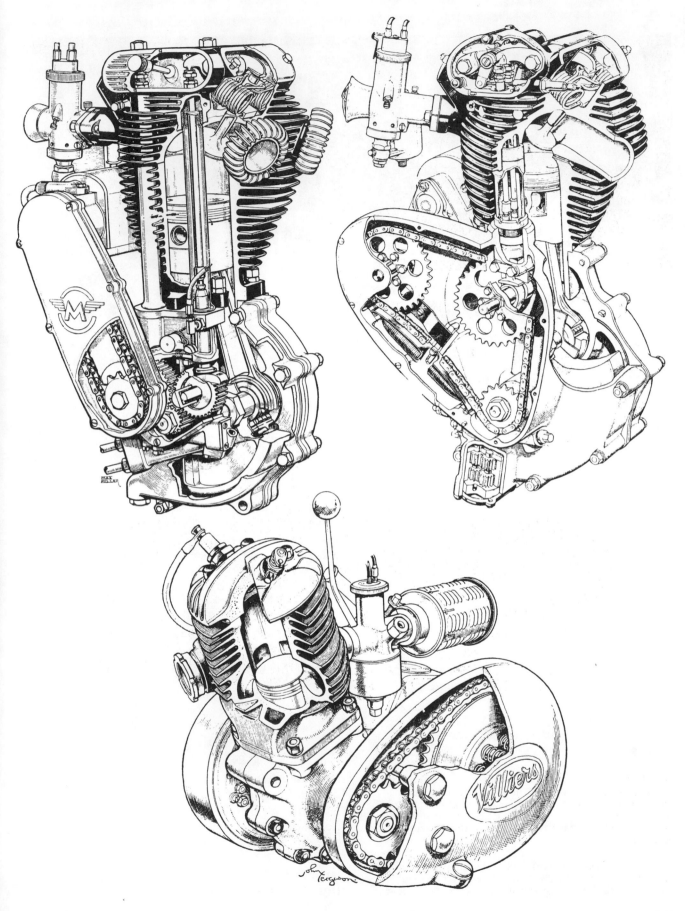

Top: BSA's 'cooking' 495 cc ohv single was renamed Silver Star for 1939. Here we see it in prototype form, the production models having a circular metal tank badge bearing a star motif. Colour details: chrome plated tank with silver top and side panels outlined with thin red and thicker black lines

Above: the block-letter tank badge identifies this as a 1939 Levis. It is, in fact, the 348 cc ohv 'A Special', a firm favourite with fans of the Stechford-based Levis factory

and the calling-up of territorials and reservists, familiar names – Cleveland Discol, Redline Glyco, ROP, Power Ethyl – disappeared from the roadside petrol pumps, to be replaced by stickers bearing the dreaded word Pool. In fact Pool was a No 3 Grade fuel of about 73 octane rating, capable of giving any engine except the most woofly side-valve indigestion. But motor cyclists had to learn to live with it,